Infidelity Recovery

A Comprehensive Workbook for Healing, Rebuilding Trust, and Restoring Intimacy in Your Relationship

Table of Contents

Introduction

Infidelity has ruined plenty of relationships. The devastating havoc it causes leaves many relationships full of potential lying dead in its murderous wake. The people from these relationships are haunted by its ghost, taunted, as they're left to wonder if they could have done something more to salvage the beautiful connection they once shared with this other person. Perhaps you, too, wonder if there's something you can do to save your marriage or relationship rather than abandon ship and mourn your losses. Here's a comforting truth. You and your significant other can save your connection using the right roadmap, sheer determination, optimism, and a desire for love to reign supreme once more.

This workbook is unlike any other on infidelity. Whether you've had your heart broken by your lover's choice to go astray or realize you've made a horrible mistake betraying your faithful partner and want to make things right again, this book is for you. It's full of practical advice, excellent worksheets, and helpful information to help you find the right path out of the maze of confusion caused by infidelity and into the brilliant warmth of a relationship full of unbridled love.

The principles in these pages are clearly outlined, leaving no room for confusion on what to do at each point in your relationship recovery journey. Allow yourself to feel relief knowing you couldn't have chosen a more effective tool to guide you and your beloved back to the joy of connection you once had. If you are both willing to set aside all pride and resistance and work through the exercises in this book together, the question of whether you stand a chance of remaining together in happiness and love will become moot. You'll find your spark once more — and it's not a matter of if, but when. So, are you ready to take back what is rightfully yours? Are you prepared to elevate your relationship beyond the zenith you've witnessed it attain? Then, there's nothing further to be said in this introduction. Begin your journey with the first chapter.

Chapter 1: Understanding Infidelity

Each night, you try to sleep, but you can't. The only thought in your mind is how the person who is lying beside you so peacefully could have made such a grotesque mockery of the trust you placed in them without question. You listen to the steady rhythm of their breath and wonder how they can find peace, especially after they betrayed you so deeply. Every time their phone rings, your heart fills with questions as you wonder what it's about. Is that another person you should be concerned about? Why are they laughing like that? Why does your partner need to leave the room to take the call? Is it someone you know? Someone you've crossed paths with before. Is the way they're looking at their phone something you should be concerned about? Or is your mind so riddled with suspicion and doubt that you're seeing shadows where there are none?

Infidelity can cause you to be concerned about what your partner is doing.
https://www.pexels.com/photo/dry-rose-flower-next-to-broken-heart-shaped-cookie-3731878/

As your fingertips gently trace the lines on your partner's face while they are fast asleep, you wonder how they could have done what they did without a moment's thought about how you might feel. You've committed yourself wholly to this person. Yet, what have you received in return? Betrayal. Heartbreak. Tears and more tears. You wish you could find it in your heart to fully forgive them. You want to give them a chance, but you can't find it in you. One moment, you've convinced yourself that you've forgiven them and let it go. Then, you're analyzing every gesture, expression, and word. The intimacy you once enjoyed with each other feels like a burden now. It's untrue. Tainted. Disgusting.

Everyone says you should forgive and forget. You want to let it go. You know you should. You feel your pain, suspicion, and hurt eating away at your insides like cancer. You want true reconciliation rather than to live with this farce. You want to heal and move past it. There's just one problem. How on earth are you expected to forgive what you can't forget? What should you do about the pangs of agony that rise unbidden unexpectedly? Is your decision to remain with this person and fix things a betrayal of yourself? What does it mean that you've chosen to stick around instead of finding greener pastures or at least being on your own? Are you that desperate? Are you terrified that perhaps no one will see any reason to be with you? Are you secretly afraid that you believe you don't deserve better and that any attempt to leave will prove you right?

These are just some of the countless concerns you have when you have been a victim of infidelity in your relationship. You desperately yearn for answers, but you're discovering there are no easy answers. There isn't a clear path forward. All that's left is the pain you feel from having your heart ripped to shreds by this person that you were so sure would always have your back as you had theirs. You know you love them, but you're also terrified that you may want to hit back. You're afraid you'll never be able to let it go and that this is the beginning of the end. Well, it doesn't have to be like that.

Infidelity and Its Many Faces

Every relationship has boundaries. Infidelity is a flagrant disrespect of those boundaries. It leads to the destruction of the trust that you and your partner have built with each other and shows disregard for the commitment and exclusivity that you share in a relationship with someone else. Infidelity destroys trust, taking only moments to ruin what may have been built over the years, decades, or a lifetime. This description of the core of infidelity may be a little too simplistic because there are so many ways that it plays out. So, to understand what infidelity is, you have to view it in its many forms. You need to peel back the layers, so you know when you are looking straight in the face of this relationship killer.

Physical Infidelity: This form of infidelity is obvious and unquestionable. There are no gray areas when your partner has chosen to be intimate with someone else or you're the one who made that mistake in your relationship. Traditionally, relationships are founded upon the concept of exclusivity, which means there are certain things that are kept between you and your partner. When you commit to one another, there is an agreement that you are the only ones who have access to each other's bodies. You enjoy physical intimacy and sexual interactions with each other and no one else. Physical infidelity can cause deep wounds that are hard to heal.

If you've experienced infidelity in your relationship, you will know all about the feeling of jealousy as you observe your partner interact with others, and you'll feel it even more so if you've attempted to patch things up. You've thought a great deal about how they chose someone else other than you. You feel humiliated because your partner's decision to step outside of your relationship to find sexual fulfillment feels like an indictment on you. It's like they're telling you you're not good enough. Once upon a time, you assumed you alone had access to their special touch, but now it's clear that's not the case. Each time they touch you, all you can think about is how those same fingers touched another person in the same way. This thought makes you question whether you are special to this person.

Emotional Infidelity: A more subtle form of infidelity, emotional infidelity can be just as hurtful. This form of betrayal is usually slicker and more insidious, so it's not easy for you to pick it up immediately. You can think of it as a slithering serpent, green and blending in with the grass. People who are unfortunate enough to be in relationships with narcissists or other similar personalities will often wonder if they have any right to be upset about this form of infidelity. Their partners gaslight them into thinking nothing is going on because there hasn't been anything physical between them and this other person.

Can you relate to this feeling? If you've ever found yourself wondering at the deep bond your partner shares with someone else, it could be that they are being emotionally unfaithful. The exclusivity in your relationship doesn't just end with sharing your bodies with no one else. Relationships are founded on vulnerability, which means you and your partner share secrets. All your hopes and dreams, fears and doubts, are the things you would never ordinarily share with anyone else. What does emotional infidelity look like? It could be sharing your worries and concerns about your relationship with someone outside of that relationship. This person isn't a regular friend, and what you're sharing isn't even something you've mentioned to your friends. On the surface, it appears as if there's nothing going on, but really, what's happening is you have begun to prioritize this person, and there is a shift in where you channel your intimacy. You begin relying on this person emotionally more than you do your partner.

Emotional intimacy could also look like flirtation. For instance, your partner may spend countless hours chatting with an acquaintance that they find interesting. You notice there's lots of laughter between them at first blush, which doesn't appear to be a problem. However, the laughter is a result of many inside jokes that your partner doesn't share with you. On top of that, these people often communicate with inappropriate double entendres. While your partner may want to insist there's nothing serious going on there, you feel you have been relegated to the sidelines in your relationship. You and your partner used to be lead actors in your relationship. Now, you've been demoted to the role of an extra.

Cyber Infidelity: Since the birth of social media, cheaters have been more creative than ever. They have countless avenues to be unfaithful to their partners. The sad capitalistic world you're in is one that actively endorses this behavior. Don't you think so? Check out the Ashley Madison scandal if you're not already familiar with it. This is a company set up with its entire business model centered on enabling people to cheat on their partners, and while it may sound like a dystopian movie plot, it is the reality of the world today. Cyber infidelity covers everything from flirtatious texting to entire affairs online. You'd think the inability to connect with a person physically should deter the possibility of infidelity. Well, think again. The Internet is a playground full of opportunities for illicit connections, riddled with traps to ruin even the happiest of marriages and relationships.

Cyber infidelity is another insidious form of unfaithfulness. What makes it even worse is that it's tough to confirm this without having to snoop or pry into your partner's business — unless divine providence intervenes and you happen to see something by accident. The paranoia from discovering cyber infidelity is so intense that even after resolving things or moving on to a different partner, you can't help but worry every time you see them on their phone or laptop. An everyday activity that is unavoidable in today's world becomes a trigger. It takes time and effort to trust that this person isn't up to no good after you've experienced this form of betrayal.

Regardless of the form intimacy takes on, it still hurts. Even if you used to be a trusting person, that trust is now utterly destroyed. At best, you decide not to suspect your partner, but your mind remains permanently open to accepting the chance that there may be something going on that shouldn't be. Infidelity leaves you confused about what could have gone so terribly wrong between you and the person you love that they had to be unfaithful. You find it hard to release your anger over their decision to hurt you in this way. Your pain and frustration blind you to the fact that sometimes, people are imperfect and make mistakes. That sentence wasn't meant to shift the blame to you or force you to forgive. You don't owe anyone forgiveness. You owe it to yourself so you can finally move on and live a full, happy life after infidelity.

Why Did They Do It?

Infidelity doesn't happen out of the blue. Certain factors create the perfect cocktail of emotions and thoughts that lead to cheating. Here's a look at some of the issues that built up to this catastrophe.

Communication Problems: At the heart of most problems in relationships is communication, or a lack thereof. Before the incident that rocked your world happened, were you and your partner struggling to communicate with each other? Did you find that countless times, rather than speak up, you'd say, "Never mind"? Is there a remarkable difference between how you and your partner communicated at the beginning of your relationship versus now? Does it feel that so many things are left unspoken or swept under the proverbial rug? When there's too much dirt beneath the rug, it's only a matter of time before one or both of you decide to look away from it completely, to pretend it's not there. When things get this bad in a relationship, some people turn to work while others will be drawn to the next shiny person. It's not every time that an unfaithful person is looking to cheat. They may want someone they can share their problems with. They want someone who understands them. If your partner could find the words, they'd tell you they were seeking connection, and that's why it happened.

A lack of communication can cause infidelity.

https://www.pexels.com/photo/man-wearing-brown-suit-jacket-mocking-on-white-telephone-1587014/

Needs Unmet and Desires Unfulfilled: When you're in a relationship with someone, you both have expectations of each other. There are certain needs that can only be fulfilled by the other person. You and your partner need emotional intimacy. Your relationship thrives when you stimulate each other intellectually. It's even better when you have passions in common because they offer you more opportunities to strengthen your bond. If you've gone too long with those needs unmet, what do you think is likely to happen? Not only is that the perfect breeding ground for resentment, but if you give in to the temptation, you'll get your needs met elsewhere. Sometimes, unfaithfulness comes from needing to fill the hunger for these desires. The unfaithful partner forgets they can communicate their need to their partner. Instead, they look outside the confines of the relationship, which is now a desert and are drawn in by the mirage of an oasis of fulfillment in the arms of another.

The Decline and Destruction of Intimacy: When intimacy in a relationship disappears, there's a storm brewing, and the fallout will be catastrophic. Why? Relationships can't survive without intimacy. Some people erroneously assume that intimacy is only about physical touch. However, there's far more to it than that. Surprisingly, it's possible for you and your partner to engage in sexual relations regularly and yet still feel disconnected from each other. How so? Realize intimacy also involves emotional vulnerability. It's about the many things you share that make you laugh and cry. When you're intimate with your partner, you both have secrets that you share freely.

However, if the intimacy between you erodes over time, you'll feel neglected. You and your partner never resolve any conflicts because it appears there's no point anymore. After all, it's not as if the resolution will lead to a reestablishment of intimacy. So why bother? This line of thinking causes one or both partners to seek a connection with someone else. It's like you're both stuck in the middle of an emotional tundra, and you're desperate for any source of warmth, even if it's only the flame of a match. You forget that if you both set aside your egos, you can create a roaring inferno of warmth and intimacy once more.

Pressures from Without, Problems from Within: If Disney had their way, life would always be happy. Everything would always be peachy. However, real life has a habit of throwing you curveballs. Sometimes, those curve balls come with so much force that they devastate everything, including your relationship. It could be a financial problem, the loss of a job, or having to take on a new job in a different location. It could be a health problem or some disagreement in the extended family that's starting to affect your relationship. Whatever the case, these external factors leave an indelible mark, and when you and your partner don't work together to mitigate the effects of these problems, it leads to a fire at home. What happens when one of you isn't present during these tough times? Being human, they'll desire comfort and solace. So, it's not a stretch to see how they may escape into someone else's arms to ride out the overwhelming storm. While handling storms by creating more storms is not a logical or effective strategy, it's the reality of life and relationships.

The Thrill of the New: Some people are unaware and unprepared for the monotony and boredom that will occasionally happen in a relationship. They expect constant thrills and excitement. So, when the initial spark dies down, they get bored. It's natural to settle down into a routine in a relationship, but for this type of person, routine feels like they're stuck in a rut. They want to break free because they feel like their life is slowly being drained out of them. These people find it inconceivable that you can remain with one person for the rest of your life. So, they deliberately engage in infidelity because they need some element of unpredictability to keep things exciting. To them, there couldn't be anything as interesting as cheating and hurting the person they claim to love. If you're the partner who's been cheated on, and this is the reason the other person gave, it can hurt like nothing else. They gave up the stability and promise of forever with you for something fleeting.

Your Emotional Journey after Infidelity

When you experience infidelity, it causes a deep wound that makes you feel unbearable pain. You may as well have been physically battered and bruised because you feel raw at the betrayal. You find yourself reeling from emotion to emotion because it's difficult to get a grip on yourself in this state of mind. When the unexpected happens, you react in the most unexpected of ways. However, here's a breakdown of what you may experience as you become aware of the betrayal.

You're in a State of Extreme Shock and Denial. The first time you discover your partner has been unfaithful, it feels as if you've had the ground pulled from beneath you. Your brain isn't entirely sure how to process this information. It was never something that entered your mind, even when you had rough times with each other. So, you find it beyond belief that this person who claims they are in love with you could do what they did. The shock is so severe that you choose to be in denial instead. If you can deny the truth strongly enough, perhaps it'll prove to be a lie. Of course, there's nothing logical about denial, and yet it's understandable because you desperately hope that this is not real. You're grasping at straws, hoping to find anything to prove this is only a cruel joke or perhaps an unrealistic nightmare.

Your Denial Gives Way to a Tidal Wave of Emotions. When you finally realize that this is real, you feel so many things at the same time. You feel grief because the relationship you thought you had with this person is gone. You're overwhelmed with anger because you can't believe this person would take advantage of your trust and love like this. Your sense of betrayal runs so deep that it causes bile to rise in your throat, burning bitter like acid. You think about your partner with the other person, and you are immediately overcome with jealousy about what they have done with each other and whether your partner made love to them in the same way they did with you.

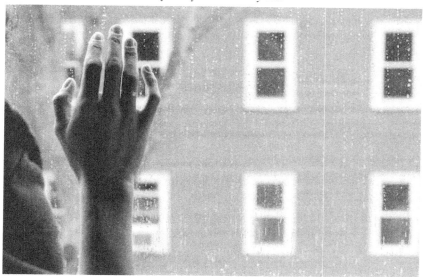

Denial gives way to a tidal wave of emotions that includes grief.

When you realize you're being jealous, you feel self-loathing. You're supposed to be mad at this person rather than feeling jealous. Your mind recalls every seemingly innocent interaction you've seen your partner have with this person, and it feels like a knife being twisted into a fresh wound, going deeper and deeper with each turn. You wonder if you were so insecure you refused to see the truth under your nose because you didn't want to lose your partner. Then you wonder if you are somehow responsible for their actions or if you're the problem because you are "not enough."

You're Overwhelmed by the Long Road Ahead to Re-Establishing Your Relationship. Your trust is gone now, and the only way to replace it is through a lot of patience and time. Your partner has expressed remorse over their actions and wants to fix things. You'd like to do the same but have no idea how to be vulnerable again. You feel like a detective when you begin regaining what you lost. You analyze every conversation and scrutinize every weird inflection in how they speak. You realize forgiveness is not something that happens instantly. It's a decision you must make each day until it finally takes root in your heart and blossoms.

Every narrative around infidelity is unique. It comes down to the individuals and the relationship with their different personalities and the dynamics of their connection. There is also the real effect of culture on the problem of infidelity. Some people have wired their minds to be ready and willing to forgive infidelity because they've accepted that people are imperfect and make mistakes. For these fortunate people, they don't have too much trouble getting over the hump. However, not everyone is so lucky. If you don't know how to navigate life after infidelity, you're not alone. It is possible, though. You can rekindle the spark once more.

The way you view infidelity depends on your attachment style, which was created in your early childhood days. If you are an anxiously attached person, you are always afraid of abandonment. So, if you've experienced infidelity, it feels like a confirmation of your fear. On the flip side, you may have trouble expressing yourself emotionally if you have an avoidant attachment style. Desperate to protect your heart, you shut down, making it hard to engage in the reconciliation process.

The Ripple Effects of Infidelity

When the stone of infidelity has been tossed into the pond of your relationship, it sends ripples that continue to travel past the spot where it sank. Here's a quick look at some of those devastating effects.

How the Betrayed Partner Is Affected:

1. They have to deal with the feelings of shock and anger. After getting over these initial reactions, the grief and pain from the betrayal are intense. The emotional laws can get so bad that they're riddled with anxiety and depression, and their self-esteem takes a critical hit.

2. Infidelity leaves a long-lasting psychological impact on the betrayed partner, inflicting PTSD. If you were the one betrayed, you become hyper-vigilant. You're constantly looking over your shoulder and terrified of becoming intimate with anyone. You may also experience flashbacks and have trouble trusting people or taking them at their word.

3. It's not only your future relationships or romantic prospects that are jeopardized. If you've been betrayed, you'll also lose trust in the people you call friends and family. You isolate yourself because the way you see it, if someone you were in love with could do what they did to you, who's to say that others aren't as deceptive? So, you isolate yourself.

4. Overcome by the emotional anguish, you may find it difficult to perform and be productive at work, which could jeopardize your prospects.

How the Unfaithful Person Is Affected:

1. If you cheated on your partner, you feel guilt and shame. You're unable to look at yourself in the mirror. Your guilty conscience leaves you riddled with anxiety. You judge yourself for making a terrible decision, and, as a result, you lose your sense of self-worth.

2. When your partner reassures you, they trust you, but you find it hard to believe. Your sense of guilt makes it nearly impossible to relax and accept intimacy in your relationship.

3. By choosing to be unfaithful, you ruin your reputation. Your family and friends may decide to distance themselves from you, and if this information makes it to your professional life, there may be repercussions.

Seeking Professional Help

There's nothing as devastating as being in the middle of infidelity. The typical response to it is to isolate yourself from the people who could offer you support during this difficult time. You would be doing yourself a huge favor by moving in the opposite direction. Even better, you should seek the help of a professional to embark on your healing journey. A professional can offer you helpful coping mechanisms rooted in actual psychology that will help you move past your pain and mental blocks toward reconciliation.

You and your partner could go for couple therapy. Why should you bother with this? Couples therapy is the perfect setup to allow you to communicate openly and honestly about your feelings with each other. The therapist will be present to mediate the conversation and ensure everyone is heard. Also, couples therapy provides you with a neutral space so everyone can focus on the root issues that caused the problem. If you decide to take this route, you and your partner have to be willing to put in the work. Recognize this is not a magic pill that will solve everything in one session. There needs to be hard work, and the process is challenging. Both of you have to draw on your reserves of resilience to pull through this dark time.

If you don't care for couples counseling, you could always go for individual therapy – a great option if your partner is uninterested in working with a professional. You have a safe space in which to be honest and process what you feel. If you're already doing couples therapy, you could tack on individual therapy as well because it'll offer the opportunity to address your problems. For instance, you may want help working out feelings of guilt, insecurity, and self-esteem problems, issues that may have led to the infidelity or worsened it.

Finally, support groups are also an excellent option. If you go this route, it's essential to choose one with an experienced facilitator who is qualified to handle infidelity. You'll love support groups because you will realize you're not the only one with your problem, and you can draw strength from others there with you.

Before wrapping up this chapter, you should know there's no right way to react to infidelity. You're a human being, and this is a complex phenomenon. So, never beat yourself up for not handling things the way you think you should have. If you were the unfaithful partner and you deeply regret your actions, you have to stop feeling sorry for yourself and channel that energy toward rebuilding the bond between you and this wonderful person who loved and trusted you. The only way to make it through this storm is by being empathetic with each other and making self-reflection a daily practice.

Chapter 2: Processing Emotions and Healing Wounds

What happens after infidelity? It would be so much easier to handle if it was a regular wound. You clean it up, bandage it, and call it a day, waiting for it to heal quickly. However, the same can't be said for infidelity. The mess it leaves behind is horrible and will require much work to sort through. You can't afford to leave your emotions the way they are. You can't suppress them because they'll come up in all kinds of ways and make it impossible to reconcile with your partner or find love in the future. You have to address them, and that's not an easy thing to do.

Many emotions can come out after experiencing infidelity.

Emotional Responses to Infidelity

The betrayed person and the betrayer will experience a myriad of feelings that can be confusing. Sometimes, they're downright contradictory. If there is to be any hope of successfully processing your emotions, you must first know what you're likely to feel in the aftermath of a relationship breakdown.

You'll Feel Furious with Yourself and Your Partner. When you think about the injustice of the situation, it makes you mad. You made vows to each other, yet your significant other had no problem breaking them. You're furious at this third party who has come between you and snatched the once-sacred intimacy. You're furious at yourself for ever daring to trust someone else with your life. Merely looking at your partner's face sends you into a tailspin of rage. What was once the face of your lover becomes the face of a snake, a deceiver who had no trouble hurting you. Your fury fuels your sense of judgment as you say you'd never do the same thing they did. Your rage may be driven by a sense of righteous indignation.

You're Overcome with a Sense of Betrayal. You were supposed to be a team, and now you aren't. Your relationship was built on a solid foundation, and now it has been utterly ruined and shattered into little pieces. All the blood, sweat, and tears you put toward maintaining a loving connection with this person have been for nothing. The memories you created as a team are now nothing more than sources of pain and anguish, highlighting the absurdity of the situation you're in and causing you to question everything, and no answer will ever be good enough.

Your Heart Fills with Sadness. The sadness comes from an awareness that the dreams you once shared are now gone. You're mourning the loss of your relationship because even if you managed to fix things, it will never be the same. You're sad because you long for the days when you could confidently say your partner would never do what they just did to you. You miss your innocence and naivete. Your partner may be right next to you, but because of their actions, it feels as if you're all alone. For the first time in a long time, you feel abandoned and have no idea what to do with yourself.

You also Feel Afraid. Your partner's actions have raised a lot of insecurities and fear in you. Does their unfaithfulness mean you are unlovable? If you forgive them and move past this, does the fact that they've done it once mean they could do it again? When they go to work, are they really going to work, or are they taking a detour to somewhere they shouldn't be? When your partner says it's daylight, should you trust their word? Sure, the sun's shining, but can you trust your eyes? After all, you trusted them once before, and look where that got you. Your mind becomes paranoid.

You Feel a Sense of Shame. Whether or not it's true, you assume people think you are the reason for this mishap. After all, why would your partner cheat on you if you weren't the cause? You start to buy into that narrative. You find yourself mulling over what you could have done to deserve being betrayed this way. The shame causes you to punish yourself. You're also ashamed that you didn't see it happening before you found out. You're not psychic, but that doesn't keep you from punishing yourself with shame anyway.

The unfaithful person isn't exempt from emotions either. Here's a quick run-through of what they'll experience.

1. They feel guilty as they remember every moment of their deception and unfaithfulness.

2. Overcome by the sudden clarity of getting caught, they feel confused about what drove them to be unfaithful in the first place.

3. They're also afraid because they have no idea what the consequences of their actions will be. They recognize there's a chance they'll lose the person they love the most and other relationships when their deception is discovered.

4. They're sad about all the times they've broken promises and lied and how deeply they've wounded their partner.

5. They're ashamed of themselves, well aware that they allowed their lesser selves to get the better of them. They can't see themselves as anything more than a destroyer of dreams, and they're humiliated by realizing what they've become.

Identifying Triggers

You could be merrily going about your business when you're suddenly hit with intense feelings over what happened because something has flung you far and hard from the present into the past. It's like you're smack in the middle of the worst of times. When this occurs, it's because you've been triggered emotionally. What is a trigger? Anything that makes you suddenly feel an intense wave of emotions reminding you of something traumatizing you've been through in your past. When you understand the many emotional triggers that could cause strong feelings, you can do something to prepare for them. You could be triggered by anything from a song you and your partner used to love to a special place where you used to have dinner or even specific behaviors you may see on television or elsewhere that your partner used to do. Triggers can hit you any place, any time, so you must be prepared.

If you hope to process your emotions effectively, the first thing you must do is identify the things that trigger you into feeling overwhelmed by them. If you don't take the time to identify the things that cause you to feel the negative wave of emotions, you leave yourself susceptible to a breakdown at any time. So, how do you identify what's triggered you? Whenever you become overwhelmed by negative emotions, you need to mentally retrace your steps and notice what you were doing or thinking right before you started drowning. Once you have identified a trigger, you should write it down in a journal to keep track of it. The following is a list of possible triggers you may have to deal with.

1. Beware of special days like anniversaries, holidays, birthdays, and other days you and your partner may have celebrated regularly.

2. You may be triggered by certain movies or songs that remind you of your partner or the affair.

3. If there are places you visited together when things were better, you may find them triggering now.

4. Did you walk in on your partner being unfaithful to you? Then trust that that area is now an emotional landmine. There's no way you won't be triggered each time you're near that space.

5. If you smell something that reminds you of your partner, that could be a trigger.

6. Specific items of clothing and jewelry could also trigger an emotional reaction.

7. Any mention of the person your partner cheated on you with is a definite trigger.

8. Social media posts that refer to your partner or the person they cheated on you with could trigger you into feeling upset. It's even worse when you see pictures or videos of them together.

9. Are there any gifts or keepsakes from your relationship? Holding on to them could trigger you into an explosive emotional reaction.

10. You may feel triggered if something in your partner's body language or tone indicates they may be deceiving you.

Sometimes, when you're triggered, it's not because of something happening outside of you. For instance, you may have intrusive thoughts that remind you of what you and your partner went through. It's not unheard of to have nightmares about this unfortunate event whenever its anniversary rolls around. You may assume you've put it behind you, but your mind hasn't. This is why it's vital to process your emotions healthily rather than attempt to suppress them.

Underlying Emotional Issues

You want to move past the problem. You'd like to get on with your life already. Yet, for some reason, you can't. What gives? It could be that you have underlying emotional issues from way back in your past that make it difficult to process your emotions after infidelity. Here's a look at some of these stumbling blocks.

You May Have Experienced a Traumatic Childhood. If you were neglected as a child or abused in any way, these are experiences that never go away. Your body grows, and your mind knows more things now than when you were young. Still, the scars remain. Nothing has changed. A traumatic childhood makes it difficult to trust people or build intimate connections with others because, in your mind, you've drawn a parallel between relationships and pain. The people you should have been able to trust as a child failed you repeatedly. They may even have abandoned and neglected you. They didn't need to use actual words to tell you that you are not worth anything to them. Their actions said at all, and you internalized the messaging. You now think of yourself as insignificant and unworthy of love. So, when the incident happened, it only reinforced what you already unconsciously thought about yourself.

Past Betrayals Can also be a Barrier to Processing Emotions. If you've experienced betrayal in any form or been deceived, it leaves you with a mark you can't wipe off. You view every interaction with the people in your life through the lens of suspicion. Since your partner betrayed you, you feel even more justified in suspecting their every move. Also, being the victim of repeat betrayals makes you feel more insecure and distrustful. These things make it nearly impossible for you to heal.

You're Dealing with Grief. You could be grieving a parent or some other relative. If you've lost a relationship that was important to you, it can put you in a fragile state of mind, making it impossible to process the pain of infidelity, let alone the confusing maelstrom of other emotions that come with it.

Your Attachment Style Is Getting in the Way. If you have an anxious attachment style, you need to be constantly reassured by your partner that they're there for you. Their engagement in infidelity is anything but reassuring, and it triggers your fear of being abandoned. Your response is to be more controlling and clingier, refusing to let your partner out of your sight. This won't do you any favors. Are you an avoidant? As someone with an avoidant attachment style, you work hard on building walls and shutting everyone out. Even a tiny little bug can find a small crevice to let it past your fences and domes! Any attempts to salvage the relationship will be countered by your desire to remain independent.

There is also the disorganized attachment style. People with this style have trouble remaining in relationships for the long haul. If you are someone who relates to this, your caregivers were not consistent in the love they gave you, as they offered you security only to take it away. You have come to expect the same inconsistency in your relationship and don't do anything to fix it.

Low Self-Esteem Makes Things Difficult. Rather than be objective and constructive in how you handle the emotions from the aftermath of infidelity, you find yourself wallowing in shame and blame. If this is your struggle, you cannot squarely put the responsibility for the relationship's breakdown where it belongs. You forget there are two people in a relationship and instead shoulder all the blame yourself. It sounds like this only affects you, but the truth is, you'll resent your partner for reminding you of how you feel about yourself deep down. So, if the two of you are to have any hope of fixing things, you have to address your self-esteem issues.

Low self-esteem can be an effect of infidelity.

These are just a few of the many underlying factors that could exacerbate the emotional damage of infidelity. The question becomes, how do you move past these challenges? It all begins with self-reflection. By making a daily practice of introspection, you'll become aware of your triggers and the other emotional issues that have remained dormant and unaddressed for years.

Tools and Strategies for Self-Exploration and Processing Emotions

Mindfulness: Mindfulness is about bringing your awareness to the present moment. By staying present, it is easier to become more self-aware and catch the thoughts and feelings that well up within you to analyze, understand, and release them. Find a quiet spot where you will not be disturbed or distracted for at least 15 minutes, and ensure you are dressed comfortably in loose clothing. You may sit on the floor or a chair or lie on your back.

Close your eyes and bring your attention to your breath. Your mind will wander to other thoughts besides your breath, and that's fine. As soon as you notice you've been distracted, all you have to do is return your attention to breathing. The purpose of this exercise is not to remain undistracted but to continue returning your mind to the present as often as it takes. You'll get the best results if you make this practice daily.

Journaling: Journaling is an excellent way to become aware of your inner world. You should have a dedicated notebook for this exercise and do it daily. The magic is in the consistency. Write about your feelings for the next 10 to 15 minutes. Don't attempt to censor yourself in any way. You can use the following questions to guide your journaling:

- "What do I feel right now?"
- "What do I think about my partner betraying me like this?"
- "What am I most afraid of?"
- "What other occurrences from my past remind me of this?"
- "What is it I need the most right now?"

Once you've finished journaling, review what you've written. Compare it to your previous entries and see if you can pick up on any recurring themes. Doing this will make you more aware of your emotions, and it'll be easier to process and let them go over time.

Mindfulness meditation and journaling are excellent tools to help you become more self-aware. Not only that, but you can also use them to deal with intense feelings of resentment and anger. If you want the best results, consider journaling straight after your mindfulness meditation.

Healthy Coping Mechanisms

If you want to process your emotions effectively, you must also take care of yourself. In other words, you must find healthy and constructive ways to release the intense feelings. Are you feeling overwhelmed? Pick something from this list and see how it helps you.

Exercise can release the pent-up anger.

1. Work out, dance, or move your body in some way that releases the pent-up anger and boosts your feel-good hormones.

2. Express yourself through art, writing, singing, or any other creative medium you love.

3. Go out and become one with nature. Rather than sit at home ruminating, go to the park, beach, forest trail, or anywhere else full of Mother Nature's gifts. You'll feel grounded after a few minutes in the great outdoors.

4. Eat healthy, and you'll do wonders for your body, which is connected to your mind. You'll think better and have more resilience to handle triggers when they occur.

5. Get good sleep. Never negotiate how long you should rest for each night. Seven to 8 hours is a good target to help you feel refreshed.

6. Be with the people who love you. Even if you're feeling raw and hurt, their presence will ground you and remind you that there's still some good left in the world. That reminder will help you bounce back whenever you feel affected by a tsunami of emotions.

7. If it all gets too much, you should seek professional help from a qualified therapist who can help you find your way through the fog and see the light again.

Emotional Check-in Guide for Couples

Whenever you and your partner struggle emotionally, you should use this emotional check-in guide to help you rebuild your connection and find firm footing with each other. Wherever you choose to do this exercise, you should not be interrupted. Setting the mood is helpful, so make it somewhere cozy and comfortable. Trying to do this exercise in glaring light could work, but adjusting the scene to encourage intimacy is far better. Also, before agreeing to this exercise, you both must ensure you have the time and that no pressing matter requires your attention. All your devices must be turned off. Remember that this period is specifically for you, your partner, and your relationship. Any notification on your phone can wait until later. Kick things off by sharing what you appreciate about your partner and let them do the same. Whatever you do, never start this exercise without gratitude. You need to positively prime each other to be receptive, open, and vulnerable, and there's no better way than clearly stating how you appreciate the other person. After this, ask each other these questions:

1. "What specific emotion are you feeling right now?"
2. "What would you like to share about how things have been for you emotionally lately?"
3. "What's the one thing I could offer you that you need the most from me right now?"
4. "How do you think I've been feeling recently?"
5. "From everything I've shared with you so far, what are the things you resonate with?"
6. "In what ways do you think we could be more supportive of each other in dealing with our emotions?"

You must be fully engaged in this exercise. Keep your eyes on each other and affirm each person's response with your body language, whether through a nod or a well-timed touch. Always remain supportive and validate the other person when they tell you how they feel, even if you feel guilty or disagree. Remind yourself that the goal of this exercise isn't to fix the other person. If you do that, you're telling them they're broken, and that's disempowering. Instead, channel your focus toward understanding how they feel and where they're coming from. Are you the sort of person who likes to offer solutions? You would be better off keeping that tendency in check and simply offering your partner a listening, supportive ear. When you've finished asking each other these essential questions, you should wrap up the same way you started: by appreciating each other.

Emotion Identification Exercise

You can't manage emotions you don't know, can you? Here's how to identify your emotions.

1. Check in with how you're feeling. If you feel several emotions, write them all down. When you've done that, put them in three groups: Positive, Neutral, and Negative. Positive emotions include gratitude, happiness, joy, ecstasy, etc. *Negative emotions* are obvious. They include anger, hate, fear, anxiety, resentment, etc. *Neutral emotions* are those of contentment, boredom, or curiosity. Write it all down in your journal.

2. Is there an emotion you're shocked to have discovered you feel? Write it down. If there is more than one, get it all out onto your journal's pages.

3. Turn your attention to your body. What unique sensations can you pick up on? Do you feel butterflies in your belly? Is your face feeling flushed? Is your chest tight, making your breaths shallow? Write down how the emotions you feel show up in your body.

4. Finally, it's time for self-reflection. Ask yourself these questions:

    a. What do you think triggered your emotions?

    b. What patterns have you noticed, if any?

    c. What could you do right now to feel better right away?

Feelings **Worksheet**

Name	Date

Think of **a prominent feeling** that you're experiencing and want to explore:

On a scale from 1 (not feeling at all) to 1 0 (most intense), **how intensely** you're feeling this right now:

Why are you feeling this way? Describe your thoughts

How does your body respond to this feeling?

How does this feeling affect your behavior?

How does this feeling affect others?

How often do you feel this way?

Do you think this is a positive or negative feeling?

If you want to change this feeling, what are some ways you can overcome it?

Chapter 3: Being Open and Honest

Do you want your relationship to thrive? In that case, you must be willing to be open with your partner. Both of you must communicate honestly with each other, and that can be difficult to do sometimes. Why? Sometimes, it's obvious that your partner cannot hear certain things without feeling hurt. However, both of you need to recognize this and set aside pride to listen to what the other person is saying. If you don't commit to this before you attempt to communicate, somebody will wind up feeling hurt, which will only compound your problems. Since you are dedicated to restoring your relationship, you must be willing to practice transparency. You have to communicate authentically and keep your dialogue respectful in the process. If one person feels like they can't communicate from a place of truth, this will only be a recipe for more resentment.

Being honest can help you begin solving your problems.
https://www.pexels.com/photo/colorful-honest-text-4116566/

Why Openness and Honesty Matter

Openness and Honesty Are the Only Ways to Build Your Trust. Anything else shatters the confidence you have in each other. If you want this back, you have to be transparent with each other. There's no room for guesswork. You both have to cover all your bases so no one has to guess your motives. You have to be transparent with each other at all times about how you feel. In this way, your relationship stands a chance of working out.

When You're Both Vulnerable, You Can Be More Empathetic to Each Other. It is impossible to be vulnerable when you don't communicate. Sometimes, what your partner says will be difficult to hear. However, you need to be present and actively listen to them. They owe you the same as well. You both have the right to talk about how you're hurt, what you need, and what you're afraid of without feeling like you're going to be judged. By being open and honest, you remind each other that, at the end of the day, you're both humans. You build a bridge that allows you to reconnect with each other once more.

Communicating Honestly Can Accelerate the Healing Process. If either of you feels they can't be honest about their emotions, resentment will build up. Resentment makes the wound more infected. So, choose honesty instead. When you're both honest, you can diagnose the root cause of the problem. You acknowledge the pain you've caused each other, and this is how you can process the trauma that you're experiencing and heal from it.

Openness Fosters Growth. Without self-reflection, there's no way to communicate authentically about your feelings and thoughts. Self-reflection is a process that always leads to personal growth and development. So, in a roundabout way, being open and honest in your communication will encourage you both to become better people. Therefore, you'll improve your relationship by leaps and bounds.

So now you're convinced of the necessity to be open and honest with your partner. How can you encourage each other to be authentic and vulnerable? Whatever time and space you fix for this conversation has to be conducive to the rawness of open, honest interactions. In other words, you both have to agree this is a safe space without judgment or criticism. You can be raw and honest about your feelings, thoughts, and experiences without being put down or made to feel invalid.

Transparency is a two-way street in your relationship, so no one should be doing the emotional heavy lifting here. You're in this together. It's up to both of you whether the ship sinks or remains afloat. So even if you are not the person who stepped outside the relationship or marriage and betrayed it, you also owe it to your partner to let them share their thoughts and feelings.

Barriers to Open Communication

You should be aware of the obstacles you will likely face when you attempt to communicate openly with your partner. In this way, you have effective strategies to head off those problems before they can further sink their teeth into your relationship. The following is a list of the barriers you will face and how to handle them.

1. **The Fear of Judgment:** When this comes up, reassure your partner using words and nonverbal communication. Try holding each other 's hands or comforting each other with a hug as you speak. Whenever you talk about how you feel, only use I statements so you don't leave your partner feeling worse.

2. **The Fear of Conflict:** Sometimes, people refrain from speaking honestly because they expect arguments and fights. How do you get over this fear? Both of you need to be on the same page and look at your conflict as a chance to grow and understand each other better. Adopt a "you-and-me versus the problem" mindset rather than a "you versus me" frame. Remember, you're working together to restore your relationship. So, you have to be on the same team.

3. **Past Grievances and Hurts:** Be willing and quick to acknowledge how you've hurt your partner. Don't make any attempt to sweep your wrongdoings under the rug. You may feel upset because they're bringing up something you thought was already resolved. However, don't dismiss them by telling them it was a long time ago. Instead, gently talk about what happened. Acknowledge your part and apologize again if needed. When you do this, you can remove those past issues from the present and not worry about them clouding the current conversation.

4. **Emotional Outbursts:** Sometimes, things may get heated between you as you share your honest opinions and feelings. The best strategy is to schedule a timeout. It would be a good idea to have

a safe word – something neutral that you can say to each other whenever you feel you're about to lose control of your emotions. This way, before you can say or do something damaging as a result of your wild emotions, you step back from the conversation and cool off.

5. **Low or No Trust**: Unfortunately, this problem has no immediate fix. You can rebuild trust by consistently being honest and following through on your promises. This will require time and patience from both of you.

6. **Different Styles of Communication**: If you're the kind of person who prefers a direct approach, you should let your partner know. The same applies to your partner. Have you noticed that either or both of you prefer a softer way of communicating difficult truths? Then go easy on each other.

These strategies are excellent for when difficult questions or brutal truths have to be shared. If you remember nothing else from this section of the book, there is one thing you should always keep in mind that will ensure you remain honest and open with your partner. The secret is the willingness to be vulnerable with each other. Rather than allow your pride, anger, or pain to cause you to build up walls, you should do the courageous thing and tear down the obstacles between the two of you. Vulnerability is about sharing aspects of yourself that the other person may not like but trusting that they will still love and accept you as you are. You know that what you share can be used to hurt you. Yet, you set your pride and ego aside for the sake of your love.

Here's a story of Layla and Kevin: Months after Kevin had betrayed Layla by having an affair, there was clearly some resentment between them. Things eventually hit a breaking point, and the two clashed. Layla was frustrated because Kevin refused to tell her everything, leaving her to use her imagination. Also, Kevin wasn't telling her he was ashamed of himself, and that's why he wasn't speaking about it. Layla would eventually find the courage to be vulnerable. She told Kevin she wanted to know everything because it tore her apart not knowing. She told him she would make peace with his answers even if they hurt. She helped him understand they could finally find freedom and peace by sharing the truth.

Kevin dared to reciprocate Layla's vulnerability by answering every question she asked. It wasn't easy to sit there and listen to him. She ran the entire gamut of emotions, from disbelief to anger, shock, and pain. However, she finally understood. By the end of that conversation, Kevin and Layla looked at each other with new eyes. After many months of pain, anguish, and resentment, it became evident to them that their love was still there and could be nurtured back to full health. However, they'd never have known this if they hadn't been willing to finally be vulnerable.

The "I" Statement Exercise

You and your partner need to pick one instance from the past where you communicated terribly with each other because of the unfaithfulness that has rocked your relationship. Then, follow these instructions:

1. Each of you needs to reconstruct the argument in writing. This time, however, you will state your points using "I" statements. In other words, rather than saying, "You made me so mad when..." or using language that indicates you're attacking or blaming your partner, rephrase by writing, "I felt so mad when..."

2. Have the same conversation again, but use your revised statements this time. Ensure you sound assertive yet calm.

3. If you have anything further to add to the conversation, remember to keep using "I" statements.

Discussion Time: Take Turns Answering These Questions

1. Did you find these "I" statements made it easier to express your feelings?

2. What changes did you notice in the tone of the problematic conversation from before versus now?

3. How do you think these "I" statements can help when you're communicating with each other in the future?

Role-Playing Conflict Resolution Exercise

You'll need a timer and two chairs placed opposite each other.

1. Pick a specific situation that often causes arguments or conflicts in your relationship. It may or may not have anything to do with infidelity.

2. One of you has to act as yourself, while the other acts as a neutral third party observing them. Set your timer for two minutes.

3. Play out the problematic scene, but use "I" statements as you speak honestly this time. The point of this exercise is not for you to win a debate or a prize. It's to practice how to effectively communicate your thoughts without causing harm to the other person.

4. If you're playing the part of the neutral observer, you have to pay active attention. Rephrase what the other person is saying in your words to ensure that you are clear on their meaning. Is there a point that has you confused? Ask questions until you gain clarity on their driving emotions and motivations. No interruptions, please, and you can't make judgments either.

5. If things devolve and become too heated, you can take time off from this exercise and try again in a few minutes.

6. When the timer goes off, switch roles.

7. At the end of this exercise, you both need to discuss how participating felt. What was it like observing from a neutral standpoint? What was it like sharing your opinions using "I" statements? Compare notes with each other. See what new things you have learned; what communication patterns in your partner have you now seen? Brainstorm to come up with different ways that you could approach conflict in the future.

You and your partner can restore the trust and love that you once had for each other. In fact, it's there, but you just need to discover it, but there's no way to tell if you don't do the work. You have to commit to being open and transparent with each other. You also have to make peace with the fact that sometimes transparency means you will get hurt. In those times, remind yourself that the only way to grow individually and as a couple in a relationship is to use the feedback to develop the union you desire. You must be patient with each other because your trust will not be rebuilt in a day or even a week.

Before wrapping up this chapter, one more thing must be said: If you're the guilty party, refrain from being frustrated with your partner because they cannot always let go of the pain. Even if you assume that your infidelity happened a long time ago, you have to remember that for your partner, the discovery is fresh. So, give them the grace of patience and time.

Chapter 4: The Healing Path to Forgiveness

After infidelity, you and your partner need to heal individually and heal your relationship together. It is impossible to heal and move forward if there is no forgiveness. Forgiveness isn't only a matter of the wronged person forgiving the offender who stepped out of the relationship or marriage. It's also about forgiving yourself, whether you're the perpetrator or the betrayed. As the person who was cheated on, you may not think you need to forgive yourself, but you have to do some self-reflection to be sure you're not blaming yourself for what happened. Unfortunately, it's not uncommon for people who have been cheated on to take on blame and shame. If you continue journaling and mindfulness meditation, you will discover if you hold any anger or resentment toward yourself for what happened.

Forgiveness can help you heal.

On the flip side, if you're the one who trashed the vows of your marriage, you will feel terrible about yourself. You clearly have your work cut out for you, as you need to acknowledge your human imperfection and forgive yourself before you and your partner can move past this. If either person in your relationship has trouble setting themselves free from self-blame, it will be tough to heal and move on. Unforgiveness, whether of your partner or yourself, will always rear its ugly head, reminding you of the painful incident and refusing to let you out of its grip. Therefore, there's no escaping the work of forgiveness if you both want to return things to how they were, or even better, between you.

What Is Forgiveness?

Imagine you're at the base of Mount Everest. You're wearing nothing but a sleeveless top and beach shorts. Your feet are clad in flip-flops. You have no food, no water, and no equipment. You have one task: to climb the mountain before you, as you are. If you don't, there will be terrible consequences. That's how difficult it is to forgive after infidelity. Fortunately, unlike the scenario you've just imagined, it's not impossible. So, what does it mean exactly? Forgiveness isn't about forgetting. Asking people to forget the wrongs they've experienced at the hands of others is unfair and impossible. There isn't a magic delete button in your brain that can get rid of specific memories. Also, certain things will trigger the memory of what happened. Does the fact that you remember those things occasionally mean that you haven't forgiven your partner? Absolutely not. This fact has to be stated right now so you don't erroneously assume you haven't forgiven this person because you can't forget what happened.

If forgiveness isn't forgetting, what is it? It's a deliberate, conscious, continuous choice to release the anger and resentment you feel against yourself or your partner. The key word is continuous. Forgiveness is a skill. How do you master a skill? Every skill in life can only be mastered through consistent practice. Some people would have you believe forgiveness happens all at once. If you accept this logic, you'll find yourself frustrated. It is a gradual thing. If you commit to the process one day at a time, you'll discover you no longer hold any grudges against your partner or yourself. You'll know you've accomplished it when you finally feel at peace.

The Psychological and Emotional Dimensions of Forgiveness

Developed by Professor of Psychology C. Raymond Knee and Kristen N. Petty of the Department of Psychology, Oregon State University, Corvallis, implicit theories of relationships are key discoveries in the psychology of relationships. They are a critical part of how forgiveness works in the context of infidelity. There are two ways you could look at your relationships.

1. Destiny beliefs
2. Growth beliefs

If you have destiny beliefs about relationships, you believe that things are meant to be –or *aren't*. It's similar to having a fixed mindset but in the context of a relationship. You don't think you or your partner can change. You assume that every relationship has its set of problems, and while that is true, you also think that things like infidelity are a clear sign that you and your lover are fundamentally incompatible. In other words, you don't believe the problems can be fixed. In that case, you are less inclined to try to forgive or patch things up. The more realistic choice for you would be to move on with your life. Even if you choose to remain with your partner, you're not holding your breath, expecting them to be faithful. They could be sincere about never wanting to commit the same offense again, but somewhere in the back of your mind, you're waiting for the other shoe to drop once more.

If you have growth beliefs about relationships, you know that relationships need work. Except there's no such thing as a perfect relationship. That's no excuse not to develop what you have with your partner. Your growth beliefs indicate that whatever challenges come up, they are simply opportunities to develop more intimacy and connection. So, even in the face of a challenge as difficult and painful as infidelity, you are constantly looking for ways to leverage that problem and turn it into something good for both of you. Research indicates that you and your partner have a higher chance of forgiving each other for your mistakes — including infidelity — if you have growth beliefs.

Other psychological dimensions of forgiveness include:

1. **The Quality of Your Relationship Before Infidelity Happened.** If you and your partner enjoyed a strong bond and were happy with

each other, there's a higher chance you'll pull through this.

2. **The Threat Level**: If you are the aggrieved person and you feel your relationship is terribly at risk on account of the infidelity, it will be harder for you to forgive.

3. **The Degree of Blame**: If the person is sincere and proactive in accepting blame and demonstrating remorse, there is a higher chance that you will forgive them. The person who cheated must take responsibility, not just in words but through actions.

Worksheet: Identifying Your Relationship Beliefs

Part 1: Self-Reflection

Instructions: You and your partner need to do this exercise individually. First, read the following statements, then pause to consider them thoughtfully. When you're certain of your true sentiments, rate how much you agree with each statement on a scale of one to five, with one being "strongly disagree" and five being "strongly agree."

1. I believe that this relationship was destined to happen.

2. I believe this relationship could become better with time and effort.

3. I believe having to put in effort to make a relationship work is a clear sign it's not supposed to be.

4. I believe that every relationship needs work and has to be nurtured for it to be successful.

5. I believe every problem or challenge I encounter in this relationship is a clear sign it should end.

6. I believe all the problems I experience in my relationship with my partner offer a chance to grow and improve together.

Scores: Statements 1, 3, and 5 are destiny belief statements, while statements 2, 4, and 6 are growth belief statements. Look at the score separately for each set of statements. The higher of both results will show you whether you have destiny beliefs or growth beliefs.

Part 2: Discussion

Instructions: Once you and your partner have finished with the first part of this worksheet, it's time to discuss the answers you have to the following questions:

1. Do you have growth beliefs or destiny beliefs?
2. What were the statements you strongly disagreed or agreed with, and why?
3. How have you noticed your beliefs about relationships affect how you react to the problems you face?
4. In what ways might your beliefs affect your ability to forgive unfaithfulness?
5. Are you willing to change some of your beliefs or work on them? If so, what beliefs do you want to adopt instead?

Remember that the goal of this worksheet is to help you and your partner understand each other and communicate clearly. No one is right or wrong for having different beliefs from the other person. Also, it's fine to change what you believe with time rather than right away. The point is for you and your partner to work together on your relationship and strengthen it.

The Benefits and Transformative Power of Forgiveness

While there are many reasons to forgive each other in a relationship, infidelity is one of the toughest problems to navigate. It is a cardinal sin; forgiving it can feel like moving a mountain with your hands. Fortunately, facts trump feelings, which means even though forgiving is impossible, you can do it. You should want to forgive because there are many benefits to letting go. If you think this process is about letting the other person off the hook, there's more to it than that. Forgiveness is about dropping your burden so you can breathe easy and live a blessed and fulfilling life.

Do you want to have happiness and peace of mind once again? Then, you need to forgive your partner for their infidelity. If you refuse to let this go, it will also taint your relationships with other people. Forgiveness is about demonstrating to yourself that no matter how badly someone has treated you, you can pick yourself back up. From this powerful position, you have no trouble relating and connecting with other people in your life because you know even when they slip up, you can trust yourself not to hit rock bottom and stay there. So do this for the sake of all the other connections that you value. Forgive yourself for this, if for no other reason. Know that anytime you're offered the opportunity to forgive someone of a transgression, you have the chance to grow in resilience and strength.

The following is a list of benefits of forgiving infidelity:

1. **You and Your Partner Have the Chance to Grow Together.** By choosing to forgive your significant other, you offer each other a clean slate from which you can rebuild the relationship. You discover the depth of the love you share.

2. **You Regain Your Trust.** While this isn't an automatic process by deciding to forgive your partner, you are saying that you'd like to reestablish a connection and work toward trusting this person again. If your partner is sincerely sorry about how they've wronged you, they will take this olive branch and work hard to show you they can be trusted.

3. **You'll Get Closure.** Holding a grudge in your heart for so long without closure does no good. Forgiveness offers you the opportunity to release the guilt, shame, and hurt so you can turn your attention to creating a beautiful future that isn't saddled with the weight of past mistakes.

4. **Forgiveness Is Wonderful for Your Mental Health.** Whenever you hold a grudge against someone, even if it feels righteous and justified, you only poison yourself spiritually and mentally. By choosing to let go, you drop all the stress of feeling like you've been wronged. You pump the brakes on the negative thoughts that nag you daily as a result of this injustice you've experienced. Compare negative thoughts to positive ones; you'll find the former is a burden to bear and the only ones that ever weigh you down.

5. **You Can Develop Better Intimacy.** When you forgive, it's saying to your partner that you want to start over. It's releasing all the terrible emotions that keep you from connecting. Forgiving automatically makes you want to better understand each other's feelings and thoughts. As a result of the mutual understanding you've developed, it's only natural that you become more intimate with each other. The bond between you will grow even stronger, so you never have to worry about repetition. You have to admit it would be so much easier to be with someone who you are certain would no longer hurt you that way than to have to start afresh with someone else who you are uncertain of because

you need time to get to know them.

It should be immediately apparent to you how these benefits of forgiveness transform your relationship for the better. Think of the best times that you had with your partner before the infidelity occurred and realize that things can be even better than that now — only if you are willing to be courageous and take the steps required to let go of the past. Having said that, it is pointless if the person in the wrong is not prepared to do what it takes to fix your relationship. If you find yourself in this situation, you should still be willing to forgive them regardless of their lack of remorse but prepared to completely let go of the relationship, as your sense of self-worth must be guarded at all costs.

Worksheet: Grasping the Importance of Forgiveness

Write your answers in a journal to make the most of this worksheet. This way, you can reflect on them later.

Part 1: Appreciating the Effects of Forgiveness

1. Think about how you've been doing emotionally. In what ways do you think your ability to forgive could help you feel better than you do? How do you think your emotional and mental health may be boosted by choosing to let go of the hurt and resentment in your heart?

2. What is the current state of your relationship? How can forgiveness help you and your partner develop a deeper connection?

Part 2: Are You Ready to Let Go?

1. Take some time to reflect on how you feel about the infidelity. On a scale of one to 10, how prepared are you to forgive this person you promised forever to? Make a list of all the things you think stand in the way of letting go of their mistake; then, reflect on how you can overcome those hindrances.

2. Set some time aside to speak candidly with your partner. Let them know about the concerns and fears you have that make it hard for you to be willing to forgive them. As you discuss with them, weigh up how remorseful they are and what they've done so far to show you they want to fix things. After your conversation, journal how you feel about whether or not you

sense they are genuinely prepared to rebuild the trust they destroyed.

3. Check-in with trusted family and friends. Sometimes, the pain you feel may make it impossible to see through the confusion from this sudden change in your relationship. If that's the case, you should be willing to seek guidance from your people. Your therapist will also have valuable input to offer you. Once you've checked in with them, consider the insights you've gained from your conversations with them and journal about how they may help or hinder your ability to forgive.

Repentance, Forgiveness, and Reconciliation

Repentance, forgiveness, and reconciliation are all inextricably linked. It is far easier to forgive when someone who has done something wrong is obviously very sorry about it and willing to do all they can to repair the damage they've caused. In other words, repentance is a show of remorse because the wrong party truly understands the impact of their actions on you. They seek to repair, mend, and bind the wounds in the hope that they can heal. When you're in a situation where your partner isn't remorseful about what they've done, it's easy to feel resentment toward them. However, in this case, forgiveness is the better option, not for them, but for you. In such situations, your decision to forgive them isn't because you intend to let them do the same thing again or get away with it but because you care for yourself. By choosing forgiveness, you set yourself free to move on from the hurt and pain and prioritize your joy.

While forgiveness happens on the inside, reconciliation is on the outside. It is a two-person job in the context of your marriage. You and your partner work hard to build the trust desecrated by infidelity. The reconciliation process means you can't afford to keep secrets from each other anymore. You have to be open and honest with each other, as you've already learned. Neither of you can afford to hold back on your concerns and fears, so you have to be vulnerable.

Reconciliation requires a painful conversation about the truth behind why what happened. It means each of you has to be willing to be held accountable for your part in the deterioration of the relationship. The best premise to have this conversation on is one where you're both open to listening to each other, even if you don't quite agree. Being defensive does not help the reconciliation process because you invalidate your partner when you argue their points. The reconciliation process focuses on brainstorming solutions to help your relationship become more resilient and impervious to infidelity or any other problematic storm that could happen to rock it.

It is possible to forgive without reconciling. However, if there is to be reconciliation between you, there must be forgiveness. If you're both on the same page about wanting to pick up the pieces and start afresh, then remorse is not optional. Remorse isn't about using flowery words to talk about how sorry you feel and how you'll never do the same thing again. It is about putting your money where your mouth is and taking action to show your partner how truly sorry you are and how desperately you'd like to repair your connection.

Worksheet: Stages of Forgiveness

There are various models with different stages of forgiveness. Forgiveness is a very individual process that depends on who's forgiving, their life experiences, the factors surrounding their marriage or relationship, etc. However, no matter the forgiveness model, certain themes pop up repeatedly because experts have identified them as the most crucial stages to true forgiveness and release. When you're ready, go through this worksheet. Take as much time as you need, and take breaks in between if you find you're emotionally overwhelmed, okay?

Stage 1: Acknowledge the Hurt

1. Do you recognize you've been badly betrayed and hurt? Don't be quick to answer this one, even if the answer is obviously a resounding yes. When you've reflected and written your answer down, think carefully about the various ways you may be attempting to suppress your pain or downplay what has happened, whether in your thoughts, words, or actions. Write it all down.

2. Describe in detail what happened. Get a factual play-by-play of the infidelity on paper, and don't be afraid to be specific and clear. This will help you acknowledge the extent of the damage.

3. Next, acknowledge your hurt. You have to look at how this affair has affected you. What are the effects on your emotional well-being? Do you feel lost, paranoid, or betrayed? What about your physical health? Are you having trouble sleeping or eating? How has this affected your connections with others? Write every way

you've noticed the infidelity has affected you.

Stage 2: Consider Everything

1. Journal about the state of your relationship before the affair. This is meant to help you see circumstances that may have pushed your partner to it. Avoid wasting your energy playing the blame game or judging your partner because the goal is to understand what may have driven them unfaithful. Replay things from their perspective, too.

Stage 3: Accept Reality

1. Realize that the infidelity did happen, and there's nothing that could change that fact. Write about how it's best to accept the truth of what occurred.

2. This step requires setting your journal aside and allowing yourself to feel the full brunt of your emotions. Let these emotions flood your mind and body. Why? You can't release them otherwise. They're ugly, but fully experiencing them is necessary in order to forgive. You can set a timer for ten minutes before going on to the next step.

3. Realize you alone are responsible for your feelings. Yes, this sounds harsh because your partner's actions triggered these difficult emotions in the first place. What happens now, though? You alone can decide to heal.

4. In your journal, commit to accepting that you cannot control the past or your partner's choices in the future, but you can control how you respond to this event. This is where you figure out whether you want to forgive them, fix things, or forgive them and move on with your life. Either way, you must release your propensity to hold on to the past and commit to moving forward. Don't assume you're no longer supposed to feel hurt or betrayed from this point on; instead, you're deciding to take back your power from this event in the past and dictate how your life will proceed from this point on.

Stage 4: Determine What's Next

1. This is a visualization exercise. Picture your life five or ten years from now. Pretend to be a fly on the wall, watching you and your partner interact in an everyday scene. Then, imagine your partner leaving the room, and you materialize before your future

self. What does your future self have to say about your decision to stay with your partner?

2. Here's another visualization exercise. You're five or ten years in the future this time, and you're not with this person. What is your future self up to? How do they seem? Materialize in front of them after observing what their life is like. What does this version of your future self have to tell you about your decision to let your partner go?

3. Journal your experiences in both visualizations and then take some time to consider your next course of action, understanding that regardless of your choice, you should forgive them for your own sake.

Stage 5: Repair the Relationship

1. As the hurt person, if you choose to forgive, you have to draw up an action plan for the process. First, journal about how you can encourage open communication between both of you.

2. There's no fixing things without getting clear on your boundaries. So, what are the boundaries you can set for yourself to maintain your sanity and emotional well-being through the repair process? Also, what are the boundaries you want to set for your partner to help fix things, and how can you communicate them clearly and respectfully? Make a plan to determine your partner's boundaries for you, if any.

3. Ask yourself what your partner could do to help in the trust-building process. Consider ways you can help as well.

Stage 6: Learn from the Experience

1. Talk with your partner to see what they've learned about the experience. Journal about it, and share your insights on the whole issue up to this point.

2. From the insights you've gleaned, what ways do you think you could prevent this problem from rearing its ugly head in the future? Have your partner brainstorm ideas, too, and share your plans with each other.

Stage 7: Forgive

1. This is when you commit to forgiving your partner, remembering it won't happen in a day, nor does it mean you'll never remember it. It's simply a decision that each time resentment,

anger, sadness, or betrayal wells up within you, you'll seize that as an opportunity to release more of the darkness and heaviness until you're lighter.

Worksheet: Reconciliation

Use your journal, as always. These exercises are for both partners but should be done individually first before you share your answers.

Part 1: Why Do You Want Reconciliation?

1. What are all the reasons you'd like to reconcile with your partner? Go into as much detail as you can in your journal.

2. What would you like to experience as a result of initiating and sticking with the reconciliation process?

3. Are there any possible stumbling blocks you're worried about tripping over as you try to mend things with your partner? Write about them in detail.

Part 2: How Do You Talk to Each Other as You Reconcile?

1. Draw up a plan of action about how you'll share how you feel with your partner and what you expect by choosing to be vulnerable with them.

2. Now, with your plan in hand, could you come up with some ideas to keep the communication between you and your significant other flowing honestly and openly as you reconcile? Write it all down.

3. When you and your partner inevitably butt heads with each other or don't see eye to eye, what's your plan for how to handle those difficult times with as much love as possible and to keep the fallout minimal at worst or nonexistent at best?

Part 3: How Do You Forgive Yourself and Your Partner?

1. Write in detail about forgiveness as you see it, both for your partner's actions and your own.

2. Now, what actionable steps could you take to encourage the energy of forgiveness to flow freely in your relationship?

3. When you're in the middle of a resentful or angry moment, how do you handle it? Could you draw up a list of things you could do to keep your focus on your desire to forgive and reconcile? Do that right now, and refer to this plan when the bitterness hits

you out of left field.

Part 4: How Do You Rebuild Your Trust?

1. What should your partner do to restore your trust in them and the relationship? If you're the one who broke the trust, what things do you think you could do to mend your partner's confidence in you?

2. In your opinion, what are the best milestones to track how well you're both doing in building trust and loyalty?

3. This isn't an easy one, but it's necessary. What do you intend to do if trust is broken once more during the reconciliation process?

Part 5: What Happens After?

1. When you and your partner finally reconcile, how do you see your relationship compared to this rough, uncertain period?

2. Are there specific changes you strongly desire to see once you've moved past the problem of infidelity?

3. Now, you need to write a commitment to your partner about how you'll deal with any similar situations or temptations that could lead to another break of trust in the future.

4. Finally, if you were the one who was betrayed, write a commitment to yourself about what you'll do the next time you find your trust has been broken. If you're the one who broke the other's trust, write a commitment to yourself about how you'll handle any situation like this in the future and nip it in the bud rather than hurt them again.

When you've finished, you can share your worksheets and discuss anything that stands out to you as worth exploring further.

Worksheet: Building Empathy

Step 1: Create an Environment That Feels Safe for Both of You. This should be quiet, without disturbance, distractions, or devices. A safe space also means not feeling the pressure of other obligations like work, so you're both in a serene state of mind and can focus on being in the here and now. So, you'll both have to agree on a time and place and commit to being there for each other to make this exercise successful.

Step 2: Talk about All Your Feelings, One after Another. You'll need to take turns and can't afford to be less than honest. However, don't assume being honest gives you carte blanche to disrespect the feelings of the other human before you. So, as you share how you feel, ensure you're using "I" statements, owning your emotions and responses rather than placing them on your partner's shoulders — regardless of whether they cheated on you or not.

Step 3: Listen to Each Other Actively as You Share Your Concerns, Feelings, and More. Your attention should be on what your partner's telling you and not the goal or working out what to say in response. Your goal is to understand them, and that means you shouldn't interrupt or let your mind drift. Your partner will feel safer sharing if you indicate you're listening through brief sounds of affirmation, nodding, or other body language.

Step 4: Reflect on What You've Learned and Offer Sincere Validation. Reflect on what they've shared with you because this shows your partner you're listening and makes them feel validated and safe. For instance, you could tell them, "What I'm hearing is you feel deeply betrayed and hurt, and the pain you feel is beyond describable."

Stage 5: Demonstrate Empathy. When you put yourself in their shoes and see through their eyes, it's not hard to empathize with how your partner feels. Do this, and then say something to show them you understand why they feel how they feel. Acknowledge your part in triggering these difficult emotions within them.

Step 6: Now, It's the Other Person's Turn. Repeat steps one through five. When you've done that, you could wrap up with a hug and thank each other for taking part in this exercise despite how difficult it is.

Chapter 5: More Trust-Building Tools

After infidelity, the process of building back the trust you and your partner once had is arduous and takes a fair bit of time. You have to be willing to commit yourself repeatedly before you can see results. This chapter seeks to help you with the best tools, advice, and exercises to help you pull your relationship back from the precipice and possibly take it to even greater heights than you both thought possible. First, you should know what trust is really about.

Trust is the foundation of any relationship.
https://www.pexels.com/photo/person-wears-multicolored-blazer-928199/

What Is Trust?

No relationship can exist without trust, and expecting a relationship to do so is like expecting a body to live without a heart or life to continue without water. Trust is the sole reason intimacy is possible. Without it, you can't feel secure in your relationship, and you'll have trouble understanding each other. When there's trust, there's vulnerability, which feeds the closeness you have with each other. This willingness to be vulnerable is why getting betrayed hurts so badly because the idea behind trusting and being trusted is you can both share the bits of yourself that no one else gets to see. So, to know that all that safety has been threatened by infidelity makes it tough to trust again. Trust, in a nutshell, is the willingness to strip off all the masks and costumes you've put up to get along with everyone in society and to lay yourself bare, warts and all, for someone else to see and accept you as you are without judgment or criticism.

Frequently Asked Questions about Trust

Q: "Can I ever trust again once I've experienced infidelity?"

Yes, it's absolutely possible. You may feel like your inability to forget what went down means your ability to trust is shattered, but that's not the case at all. You can rebuild the trust between yourself and your partner, and by putting what happened in the correct perspective, you'll find you don't have trouble trusting. If anything, you'll be inspired to take a critical look at your connections with friends, family, and colleagues and see how you can encourage more openness and honesty by demonstrating your willingness to hear people out, even when the truth is ugly.

Q: "Is it possible to trust my partner, considering they've cheated on me?"

You have the ability to trust them. Sure, it will require your partner to show you they're also well aware of what they've done wrong and putting in the effort to reassure you that their mistake is a one-off. It will also require bravery on your part by being willing to meet them halfway, giving them the benefit of the doubt. You'll both need to be more open than you've ever been with each other, but you can swing it.

Q: "How long will it take me to build back my trust once I commit to the process?"

The process will take as long as it takes since every couple who struggles with the effects of infidelity is different. Generally speaking, the process could take months or even years, depending on how eager you are to mend things.

Q: "If the person I love truly loves me, why did they break my trust in the first place?"

Many factors contribute to people making poor choices like cheating, which affect their relationship or marriage for worse for a long time. However, you should know it's not your fault that your partner cheated. It would be unfair to take responsibility for damage you didn't cause.

Q: "Is it a cause for concern that I'm struggling with trust after my partner's unfaithfulness?"

No. It's perfectly normal and a natural response to being betrayed. If someone's making you feel like the bad person for not being able to trust your partner right away, they're wrong. *You don't need that sort of toxicity in your life.*

Self-protection after betrayal is a natural protective mechanism. When ancient humans tried new plants and fruit as they foraged, they would find out that not everything that looked edible should be eaten. Therefore, they were more careful and did all they could not to eat things they'd confirmed were poisonous. Whenever they came upon similar plants or fruit resembling the ones that seemed poisonous, what did you think they did? They were *cautious* because they remembered what had happened previous times. However, they didn't lose their trust; humans would have rather limited food options than no options at all! The point is that it's natural to be mistrustful, cautious, and hesitant to let your guard down when someone has hurt you. You're justified in feeling this way — but realize it doesn't have to last forever and shouldn't because that would be poisonous to your well-being.

Q: "Why do I feel so ashamed and foolish for wanting to rebuild the trust between myself and my partner since they had no trouble doing what they did?"

You may be considering what others may think or feel about your decision. While your friends and family will offer advice from a place of love and concern, at the end of the day, you're the one who decides whether or not to pull the plug on your relationship. If anyone judges you for choosing to repair and rebuild, that's their problem. They aren't you, so there's no way they'll know the nitty gritty about your relationship with your partner. You don't have to feel ashamed, and you shouldn't think of yourself as a fool. You don't have to explain your decision to anyone if you don't want to.

Q: "Will I be able to salvage trust after this?"

You can, and if you both can be honest and open while working hard at it, you will. Once more, it's a long process, but the good thing about processes is they will bring you to an expected end as long as the two of you work on this like it's a project and you're a team.

Now you have the answers to some of the most frequently asked questions regarding infidelity and rebuilding trust, it's time to get to work on repairing the damage.

Trust-Building Tools for the Unfaithful Partner

Tool #1: Complete Transparency. If you want to show your partner you can be trusted, you must be transparent about everything. If you've been transparent in the past, your goal is to go above and beyond everything you've ever done to stay open and clear about your thoughts, intentions, whereabouts, choices, etc. You may assume that transparency is about talking about the things you did during your infidelity, but there's so much more to it than that. You must be willing to share everything about the other parts of your life — and not just what's happening now, but any plans you may have made without telling your partner. If there is such a thing as ruthless transparency, that's what you should be doing. There's no such thing as too much information after you've been unfaithful to your partner and are looking to regain their trust.

Tool #2: Consistent Behavior. Inspiring trust in your partner is impossible if you are inconsistent in your behavior. What does that mean exactly? Consistent behavior means you disclose everything about your plans and actions. If your partner asks you questions, you don't hold anything back because you feel uncomfortable. It is their right to know the answer. So, you have to answer truthfully. Your words must be backed by your actions. Otherwise, you give your partner more reason to doubt you. So, consistent behavior is about constantly showing your partner that you are committed to rebuilding trust through your actions and words. The more predictable you are, the more reliable your partner will find you.

Tool #3: Ownership of Mistakes. When you own up to your mistakes, you must have a face-to-face conversation with your partner. Obviously, you should be prepared before you tell your partner you'd like to talk to them. You must have deeply reflected on what you did wrong and how badly it hurt your partner. When you speak to them, admit your mistakes and help them understand what drove you to breach the trust you once shared. While explaining your actions and taking ownership of your mistakes, you should avoid making another mistake: being defensive or blaming things or people outside of yourself. The whole point of this tool is recognizing that you are responsible and letting your partner know that you are taking accountability for your misdeeds. If you get defensive or make excuses for your actions, you only antagonize and hurt your partner even more. Owning your mistakes is also about being committed to change. So, tell your partner how you intend to improve things, and if you care about them, follow through.

Tool #4: Actions. Flowery words mean nothing if you don't act on them. Also, taking one step does not atone for what you did wrong. Remember, you have to be consistent in your behavior. So, if you want to rebuild trust with your partner, ask yourself what positive things you can do that will demonstrate to them you truly are sorry and want to change. Do you need to manage your time better? Was the infidelity caused by a lack of bonding time between you and your partner? In that case, it would make sense for you to develop a plan of action to help you with better time management. Did you have trouble understanding your partner or communicating with them? Was this why you felt driven into someone else's arms? Do what you can to encourage openness and honesty each time you connect with your partner. If you have to take a class on relationship communication, you should do that. The point is you should show your partner that you are remorseful so your partner can see you're not all talk and no action.

Tool #5: Individual Counseling. It's possible that the things that led you to being unfaithful to your partner are problems unique to you. Whether you're sure of this or not, you'll benefit from seeing a therapist for individual counseling. If you genuinely want to ensure you never repeat this, you need to understand the real reasons you breached your relationship's trust, and there's no better way to figure out the nuts and bolts in your head than by seeing a counselor. You may be surprised to discover deeper layers of insecurity and fear that motivated you to act in a hurtful way to your partner. The good news is once you learn about these things, you can work on them to become a better person. By gaining the light of self-awareness through individual counseling, you're less likely to make the same mistake in the future.

Individual therapy can help with self-awareness.

Trust-Building Tools for the Betrayed Partner

Tool #1: Communicating and Expressing Your True Feelings Openly and Honestly. When you have been hurt, you need to be open about how you feel, not just for your sake but for the sake of the relationship. By expressing your feelings to the other person, they'll understand the extent of the damage they've caused with their behavior and are more likely to be spurred on to do more to fix things. If you attempt to suppress how you feel by telling them it's okay and trying to let them off the hook easily, you do yourself a great disservice. You need to stand up for yourself, and that means sharing how your partner's betrayal has made you feel. This doesn't mean you have to be disrespectful, rude, or vengeful in how you tell your partner. Remember, the best way to communicate if you intend to rebuild this relationship's trust is by using "I" statements to claim ownership of your feelings.

Tool #2: Setting Personal Boundaries. As a person who has been betrayed in a relationship, you need certain things in place to make you feel safe. Setting boundaries is an effective way to restore the feeling of safety in your relationship that your partner's infidelity has destroyed. Your partner may do their best to help you feel safe and trust them again. However, they are not a mind reader and may be unable to tell when they engage in certain behaviors or speech that leave you insecure and full of questions. What's better than sitting and stewing over every little thing they do? You have to set boundaries.

Let your partner know when they're doing something you find unacceptable and will no longer tolerate. Help them understand what your needs are and what you expect from them so they know not to deviate. It's much better to tell your partner your boundaries than expect them to know them. Why? When you let them know what is and isn't okay, and they still go out of their way to disregard those boundaries, you'll know for certain that you need to end things with this person who disrespects you. Your boundaries should be in line with your values. Do things like respect, love, understanding, communication, and honesty matter to you? Your boundaries should be centered on those values. It's also fine if you discover new limits to rebuild trust in your relationship. Simply communicate them to your partner as you find out about them.

Tool #3: Attend Couples Counseling. The candid truth is that you can only do so much to repair your relationship by using workbooks and watching videos. All of these tools are supplementary at best. It would be much better for you to consult a professional counselor specializing in relationship and marriage matters. You see, your relationship is unique. It is different from every other one out there. Therefore, there's only so much cookie-cutter advice can do for you. That's not to say that using this book will not work. However, to give yourself the best shot, you should see a couples' counselor to address specific issues relevant to you and your partner. Dealing with the specifics is a great way to mitigate the chances of experiencing infidelity in the future and forge a stronger, unbreakable bond between you and your significant other.

Tool #4: Setting Joint Goals. Remember, your relationship is a joint project. You cannot rebuild trust in isolation. You're a team, so you must work hard to restore your relationship to its former glory and possibly even improve it. When you come together to figure out your goals for your relationship, there is a greater chance that you'll succeed at rediscovering your love and trust for each other. You're more willing to cooperate because it doesn't feel like one person is doing the emotional heavy lifting for everyone else. Some goals you can work on include personal growth, better communication, more quality time with each other, better transparency, more patience, etc.

Worksheet: Active Transparency

Write your answers in your journal and reflect on them when you're done.

Part 1: What Does Transparency Mean to You?

1. In painstaking detail, describe what transparency means to you.

2. Consider why transparency matters to your partner, yourself, and your relationship. Write them in detail.

3. Think about the times when you haven't been above board with your partner, which has caused you and your partner to struggle with intimacy or understanding. Write about those events and how you could have handled them better by being transparent.

Part 2: Reflect on Your Past Choices.

1. Write down everything you've done in the past that your partner has no clue about. This isn't the time to censor yourself or hide anything, not if you want to return to a place of trust and peace in your relationship.

2. When you've got it all down on paper, ask yourself why you never told your partner these things, and write down your answers.

3. Finally, you will disclose all of this to your partner in a letter, ensuring you clarify that while your goal isn't to hurt them but to be above board with them, you understand that the fact you've withheld things will hurt them. Let them know you want to move forward with rebuilding your trust if they're open to it, and that's why you want to throw all your skeletons out of the closet and onto the floor.

Part 3: Get to Work on the Trust between You.

1. What do you think could make it difficult to be truly transparent with your significant other, and how would you deal with them? Write it all down.

2. Draw up a plan for regularly letting your partner know where you are whenever you're not together.

3. Write about how you think your relationship could benefit from your decision to be more transparent about where you are, who you're with, what you're up to, how you're feeling, and everything else your partner should know.

Part 4: Getting Feedback and Adjusting as Needed.

1. It's time to share your plans to be more transparent with your partner. The goal is to find out what they think about it and look for ways you can make it work together.

Worksheet: Creating a Relationship Vision Board

Did you know vision boards are not only for manifesting yachts, mansions, and material things? You and your partner can create a vision board for your relationship so you can see what you're working towards and feel motivated to accomplish your vision. Follow these steps to create the vision board that encompasses your values, hopes, and dreams for your life together as a loving couple.

Step 1: What's the Purpose of Your Vision Board?

Be clear about what it is you'd like to accomplish in your relationship because that will determine what goes on the vision board. Do you want a relationship where you have more time with each other? Would you like to be more open and communicative about everything with no holds barred? The two of you need to brainstorm as a team and share values that the other person may not have mentioned or thought of. Make sure the goals you have for your relationship are clear and achievable so neither of you feels overwhelmed by trying to do too much all at once.

Step 2: Get the Materials for Your Vision Board.

You'll need a large piece of cardboard paper or a whiteboard if you prefer. While digital apps work well, having your vision board somewhere you can see each day is much better. So, if you're going the traditional route, you'll also need old magazines or posters and photos printed from the internet.

Step 3: Find the Images and Words That Match Your Goals.

You'll need to browse through magazines, online images, stills from movies, etc., to find every word and image that lines up beautifully with the goals you've set as a couple. You could also select stills of couples from your favorite movies that embody the sort of relationship you'd love to have with each other in real life, as they capture the spirit of the dream relationship— that you'll create with your significant other.

Step 4: Arrange the Printouts and Cutouts on the Board, Then Glue Them Down.

You should work together to make it look aesthetically pleasing to both of you and be willing to compromise when you don't see eye to eye. When you both take a step back and look at what you've done, and you're happy with the results, it's time to glue everything in place. Your vision board should be something you both love to look at.

Step 5: Set Your Board Somewhere You'll See It First Thing in the Morning and Last Thing at Night.

When you can see it every time you go to sleep and wake up, it will remind you of how deeply you value your relationship and the person you're so lucky to call your own. You'll be inspired to actively seek ways to reach your goals, and your intimacy with each other will be better and better each day.

Step 6: Please Check in with Each Other to Talk about How Well You're Doing.

You can't just set up a vision board, dust your hands, and expect some Law of Attraction fairy to wave magic dust all over it and make your dreams come true. There is work to be done, and you need to check in with each other to see how far along you've come since setting up the board. Try to check in at least once a week to see where you're doing better and what could use some improvement.

Chapter 6: Restoring Emotional and Physical Intimacy

One of the things that takes a massive hit from infidelity is intimacy. The betrayed partner has trouble letting the one who cheated close, physically or emotionally. As for the ones who cheated, they struggle with feelings of self-worth because of the guilt about what they've done, and not only that, in their bid to separate the person they cheated with from their significant other in their minds, they may not want to initiate any form of intimacy. On top of that, if your partner betrayed you, they're probably struggling because they expect you to reject any attempt they make to get close to you. You may already have rejected them in the heat of your anger — not that you're to be blamed for what's a natural, instinctual response to being cheated on.

Can intimacy be restored?
https://www.pexels.com/photo/man-and-woman-holding-hands-3228726/

So, the question is, can intimacy be restored? Is it possible to want to hold and be held by this person once more? Could you find it in yourself to be vulnerable with them and share your innermost thoughts as you used to do, once upon a time that feels so long ago it's almost like it was all a dream and nothing more? Well, you'll be glad to know that you can restore the intimate connection you once had and improve on it, too. That's what this chapter will teach you. You'll discover the secrets to bringing back the emotional and physical closeness you and your partner once had. You'll find an ember that can be nurtured into a bright, roaring fire if you can fan it just right.

The Effect of Infidelity on Emotional and Physical Intimacy

Infidelity hurts so much because of the havoc it wreaks on your emotional and physical well-being, and it also affects your ability to connect with your partner intimately in every way conceivable. First, here's a closer look at how infidelity affects how emotionally intimate you are with your partner. One undeniable effect is the pain of betrayal, making wanting anything to do with the person who was so willing to cause you such deep sadness unthinkable. When you realize you've been betrayed, nothing hurts more, and you trusted this person you once thought couldn't even be on the list of people who could hurt you. Your trust is gone, and, as a result, so is your desire to be intimate. Betrayal is a traumatic experience, and when you're traumatized, it's impossible to feel safe in general, let alone when you're facing the one who broke you.

The betrayal of infidelity causes every couple to become emotionally distant from each other, and sadly, you're no exception to the rule. It is natural to feel a sense of coldness at best or repulsion and disgust, at worst, toward your cheating partner. Sometimes, the feeling gets so bad that it devolves into outright resentment. If someone had told you in the weeks and months leading to the present time that you'd one day have the sort of hateful thoughts and feelings you do toward your partner, you would have laughed because the very idea would have been ridiculous. Yet, this is an unfortunate real effect of infidelity. It's impossible to build any emotional intimacy when, on the best of days, you feel cold, and on the worst of days, you're an unstoppable volcano desiring to burn everything about your partner.

When you can't be emotionally intimate with your partner, what are the odds you'll allow yourself to be physically intimate with them? It's impossible. Even if you tried, there would be a noticeable difference in the energy and purity of intimacy from before the unfaithful act happened compared to the present, after the fact. If you tried once, you'd not be willing to give it a go again because, somehow, you feel dirty. As for your partner, they're too riddled with the shame and guilt of their choices to be truly present with you. It's uncomfortable for you both because this third person between you, while not physically present, takes up so much space between you as though they're the elephant in the room.

When you learn you've been cheated on, you feel anxious, stressed, and depressed, and sometimes, your mental symptoms can get so bad that they play out as chronic pain and other physical ailments. The last thing on your mind is getting physically intimate, and if you have to take medication for your condition, guess what? You will most likely be disinclined to have your partner touch you in any way. You may also be unwilling because of your loss of self-esteem since the natural place your mind heads to when you're betrayed is that you must not have been good enough for your partner.

Obstacles on the Path to Restoring Emotional and Physical Intimacy

The following are obstacles you will have to contend with when you are on the journey of restoring the bond between you and your other half:

1. You may make yourself too busy, not realizing that's only to distract yourself from the problems at home.

2. You and your partner may give in to the temptation to criticize each other. Usually, whatever you're criticizing each other about has nothing to do with what's really going on. Your cutting looks and remarks are really a cry for help, a call for attention, a desire to end the madness you find yourselves hopelessly drowning in, silenced by egos too big to admit their pain or to be vulnerable.

3. Impatience is another problem, as you may be less willing to put up with things you had no trouble tolerating before things went south.

4. Your perception of yourself could make it hard to be willing to reach out to the other person and others in your life.

These are just some of the barriers that could be in the way when you decide to develop your emotional and physical intimacy. You have to be on the lookout for these obstacles and be proactive about dealing with them. Otherwise, they will leech whatever love is left between you and your partner, and it will only be a matter of time before your relationship ends.

Worksheet: Bringing Back Emotional and Physical Closeness

This exercise aims to help you and your partner create the best conditions to make it easier to reestablish and strengthen your intimacy.

Part 1: For Emotional Intimacy

1. You'll need a pen and paper for this one. Together, brainstorm various things you know you both enjoy doing as a couple. Don't feel the need to make every item on your list too fancy or ambitious. For instance, if you enjoy simple things like watching a movie together, you should add that to your list. What about walking or taking a hike? Is camping something you'd both be

open to? You could also write things you've never done before as a couple or on your own and give them a go.

2. Set a schedule for when you'll do these activities, being mindful that you both need to be in the right headspace for them. It's best not to schedule things when the other person will be busy. Here's a list of things to help you get started (you can add more activities if you wish):

   a. Date nights (could be indoors or outdoors).

   b. Travel (you could go somewhere you've been together before or somewhere you've both never been but have always wanted to check out).

   c. Work out with each other. Make sure you choose something that matches both of your fitness levels.

   d. Make a meal together, whether it's something new and unfamiliar or something you're both good at.

   e. Volunteer your time to a cause you both care about. You could go to an animal shelter, for instance.

   f. Take a class on something you've both been meaning to learn.

3. After each activity, take time to think about how you feel about each other. Is there any change? Are you any closer? Write about your feelings in your journal, then share your thoughts. If you don't feel closer to the other person, don't be dishonest. Tell the truth with kindness. Also, if it turns out it's your partner who doesn't feel any positive change, you shouldn't be mad at them. Change takes time. Be patient and trust the process.

Part 2: For Physical Intimacy

Remember, you can't fast-forward your way from broken intimacy to sex. It doesn't work like that. For now, your focus should be on non-sexual touches. So, keep that in mind as you do this next part of the worksheet.

1. You have to have a heart-to-heart conversation about how you both feel regarding getting physically intimate with one another. Among the critical matters you should discuss are your boundaries. What are you comfortable with? What isn't, okay? You need to know these things about your partner, too. As always, there's no reason to rush this process. It will take as long

as it needs to.

2. Come to an agreement about the physical touch you're willing to start with. Perhaps you could manage a ten-second hug or at least hold hands for a minute. What's the point? It's to teach your bodies and minds that there's nothing to be afraid of when touching each other, to remind yourselves that once upon a time, you couldn't stand being apart and that you really do miss that. Do this daily rather than wait for the "perfect" occasion to connect. You could do this right before you go to bed, as this will help you keep your goal of restoring intimacy in your mind while you sleep. The result is it will be the first thing on your mind when you wake up, and whether you know it or not, you'll seek ways to show each other more affection. Other ideas besides hugging and holding hands include cuddling, offering each other non-sexual massages, reassuring squeezes, rubs, and pats.

3. At the end of each day, write in your journal what it felt like to be connected. Have you realized that what you interpreted as disgust or repulsion is a thin veneer for the danger you felt? Are you learning more and more that there's nothing dangerous about the other person's trust? Are you starting to get that warm glow in your heart yet? Don't worry if this doesn't happen the first week or even a month of doing this exercise. Keep going, and you'll see progress eventually.

Worksheet: Conversational Prompts

1. **What Are Your Dreams?** What do you hope to accomplish? Talk about it with each other. Share where you think you'll be in five to ten years. Be willing to be vulnerable, and never miss a moment to find your sense of humor.

2. **Now, What Are Your Fears?** What are the things that keep you up at night, your insecurities, and concerns? Listen actively and empathetically to each other, as this is a great opportunity to connect on a deeply emotional level.

3. **How Did Your Day Go?** Talk about it with each other. Listen to each other because this shouldn't be about one person stealing the show. Let each person shine. Celebrate good news, and empathize over the bad. This is how you'll connect better emotionally and, eventually, physically.

4. **Share Memories of Childhood.** Think about your favorite ones and your darkest ones. Share it all, and hold nothing back. As you do, you'll not only learn new things about each other but also have a better understanding of why you each act the way you do.

5. **Talk about the Things That Mean the Most to You,** as in the things you value the most in life, as this is another way to find common ground with each other and learn how to meet each other halfway.

6. **Next, Talk about the Things You Love the Most about Each Other.** What was it that drew you to each other? Talk about the funny things you noticed about each other in a good-natured way so there's something to laugh about. Laughing is an excellent way to strengthen your bond as a couple.

7. **Now, Talk about What You Love about Your Relationship** and what you think you could make better with a little more attention and elbow grease.

Exploring Touch Further

Touch is such a powerful way to connect with someone else. There are many ways to touch each other that don't have to do with sex but will help bring you closer to each other and show you can trust each other once more. People underestimate the range of emotions and messages that can be communicated with a simple touch. Touch your partner one way, and it shows them gratitude. Change it up a bit, and you're showing them you're feeling vulnerable. Make another adjustment, and you're offering comfort or reassurance. Done lackadaisically, it communicates a lack of concern.

So, what does non-sexual touch look like? It's putting an arm over the other person's shoulder, stroking their neck or back as you pass them, or holding their hand. It's touching your partner on the face, softly, to show them how precious they are to you. It's touching their arm gently to show your support and empathy. Whatever you choose, when you add eye contact into the mix, you exponentially increase the love and care behind those sweet gestures, tugging on the other person's emotional heartstrings while reminding yourself why you've chosen this person rather than anyone else to do this "life" thing with.

Eye contact can increase the emotion behind gestures.

How can you use touch to show your partner you care about them? You could offer them a foot massage when they're tired or just because. It's great for them as they'll feel relaxed as you touch them. A hand massage is also lovely to receive, and you can do this while you're watching a movie or being "alone together" while you're both doing your own thing in the same room. You could also hold them close, as this will feel comforting and increases oxytocin, a hormone that encourages bonding. It's called the "love hormone" for a good reason, which is why you should both hold each other for a minute or more a day to boost your trust in each other and stop being afraid. As you hold each other, your hypothalamus generates oxytocin, which tells you both that you're safe.

Did you know that when you hold each other, you also create other hormones like dopamine and serotonin? Well, why do they matter? Dopamine is called the "reward hormone," and it's the reason you're ready to work hard on something until you accomplish it. It's the reason you feel good. So, as you hug each other, you feel happy, and you'll want to touch each other more often. Naturally, this will spill over, causing you both to be more willing to be emotionally intimate. Your brain registers touch between you two as a good thing to be sought out as often as possible. Then there's the serotonin, or the "happy hormone," which is excellent for keeping your mood nice and steady. Holding each other in a tender embrace encourages your brain to release serotonin, making you feel true happiness. It feels like your body and mind are at their best, and you're both in a better position to connect.

Don't be afraid to use touch to show your partner you care if they're open to it, whether it's a cuddle, a hair ruffle, or a gentle kiss on the cheek or the forehead. You have to be attentive, too, so if you can tell they don't want to be touched, you let them be and allow them to come to you. Do you know what's even better? Asking for consent before you touch your partner. Sure, it's easy to assume that's not necessary because you're not touching them sexually, but by asking for consent, you show your partner you care about them. Also, asking shows them you're willing to be vulnerable, encouraging them to do the same with you. If there's one thing to always remember, it's this. The small gestures make the most significant changes in restoring your emotional and physical intimacy with each other. Set your ego aside, wear your heart on your sleeve, talk with each other about your action plan to restore your closeness, and don't be afraid to give it your all.

Chapter 7: Sexual Intimacy and Reconciliation

Now that you've made progress on restoring emotional and physical intimacy in your relationship, it's time to address the matter of sexual intimacy. It's going to take time and effort to get to the point where you and your partner enjoy being sexual with each other, but you can pull it off. There's no shortcut through this process. It's going to take as long as necessary. If either of you feel rushed, it will only slow things down, increase the awkwardness and discomfort, and possibly put you off the idea of sexual intimacy altogether. At this point, you need to use open communication and mutual respect as your best tools to bring back the spark between you both. Before you can conquer the challenge of a dead bedroom, you need to know how you got here in the first place. You need to know everything about how infidelity destroys sexual intimacy to reverse-engineer the process.

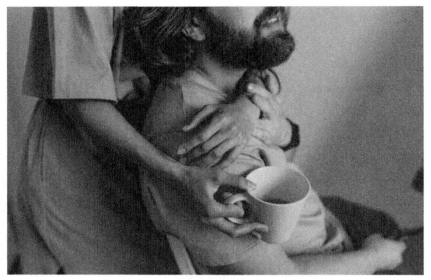

Open communication and mutual respect can bring back the spark between you and your partner.

https://www.pexels.com/photo/photo-of-a-man-being-hugged-4406725/

The Impact of Infidelity on Sexual Intimacy

An Unwillingness to be Sexually Intimate Because of Guilt: If your partner's the one who cheated, they'll have a hard time wanting to be intimate with you for several reasons, chief of them being they don't think you've forgiven them. So, they prefer not to even try. They are being eaten up from the inside by the shame of choosing betrayal over keeping your relationship. When this is what's happening, they can't even allow themselves to be emotionally intimate with you or have conversations about your feelings. If you try to initiate sex, they'll be hesitant. They can't be in the moment because they're stuck in their head, wondering how and why you could still be with them, fearful that they'll wind up pushing you away if they say or do the wrong thing. They may not even be aware of all that is happening in their minds, and, in that case, they may not even have the libido to see things through, let alone be turned on enough to want to share a bed.

A Feeling of Numbness: From the moment you learn your partner has cheated on you, a part of you dies. Everything about you that enjoyed feeling pleasure shuts down, not just in your mind but in your body as well. The reason this happens is because the discovery of infidelity is a form of trauma, and trauma always leaves its mark on body, mind, and spirit. So, when you first discover the truth and the reality of the situation hits you fully, you're in shock. Your body thinks that's because you're in trouble, so to protect you, it shuts down. It's like you get a hit of natural Novocain, and you're numb now, both emotionally and physically, which means you don't react or respond as you ordinarily would to anything, let alone sexual touch. The numbness affects every sense organ, and that includes your skin. Your partner can't look, smell, or feel good enough to get you sexually excited. Their touch doesn't do it for you anymore, and you'd rather not bother with even the most non-sexual of touches.

A Desire to Guard Your Partner: When you discover betrayal, you may become so anxious about your partner that you begin to act territorially around them, doing all you can to signal to others that they're yours and everyone needs to back off. This isn't romantic behavior, as the movies would have you believe. Instead, your desire to give in to "mate guarding" is a primal one driven by raw fear and anxiety rather than a need to bring back the love between you. By acting this way, you signal to your partner that you don't trust them not to slip up again, whether you mean to or not. This makes them feel even more ashamed and unlikely to want to engage with you sexually.

Even if you have sex with them, you'll both be able to tell it's not coming from a place of genuine desire for each other but that there's a cloud of desperation hanging over both of you. They'll also feel they're only consenting to your advances because they feel pressured. All of this causes your relationship to buckle under the weight of all these fear-driven expectations as your partner begins to resent you, even if you feel they don't have the right to since they cheated. You can see how none of this does your relationship any favors.

Intense Trust Issues: The breach of trust from betrayal makes it hard for you to want to open up or put yourself in a vulnerable position with your betrayer by allowing them access to your body. In a relationship, you expect your partner to protect and preserve your emotional safety, but then, once unfaithfulness enters the picture, it's close to impossible to open yourself up like that. You're mistrustful – and with good reason. The thought of putting yourself in a position to be fooled once more is a huge turn-off, and even when you really want to let it go, it's tough. You'll need time to recover, to break down the barrier between you and your partner that keeps you from sharing your love and affection for each other freely, without shame or guilt.

There's also the risk that even after you've forgiven your partner, they may have trouble trusting that you've let it all go. So, whether consciously or not, they punish themselves by refusing to give themselves to you fully when you're attempting to connect with them emotionally and sexually. They don't trust that you're sincere in your desire to be with them physically. They're watching you through eyes squinting in suspicion as they wait for the other shoe to drop or for the mask they imagine you're wearing to slip.

The Natural Ebb and Flow of Sexual Desire

You're human, and one of the key traits of humanity is having desires, with sexual desire being one of the most basic and important ones. It's about wanting to connect or bond with someone else through the wonderful gift of sex, and unless in an asexual relationship, it's expected that you and your partner will connect with each other this way. Sexual desire is a fundamental part of conventional relationships, determining how long your union with your partner will last. It's about more than just physical pleasure, allowing you and your partner to enjoy the feeling of loving and being loved.

The level of sexual desire is not the same all the time, as it ebbs and flows for everyone, and it's natural for you and your partner not to be as sexually active as you were with each other at the start of your relationship. You may both be advancing in years. Or, one or both of you may struggle with more stress than usual. If there's been a significant change or upheaval in your routine, sex may be the last thing on your mind, and the same applies when there are serious health issues that need to be addressed. You should never let anyone make you feel your relationship is on the rocks because you and your partner aren't going at it like bunnies. It's only natural for the dynamics between you to wax and wane with time. However, when you're not having sex because of infidelity, that's a different matter entirely and one that needs to be addressed. Infidelity can take the ebb and flow and turn it stagnant with no action at all. A dead bedroom could lead to the end of the relationship if you don't do the work to bring back sexual intimacy.

Body and Heart

There's an undeniable connection between emotional intimacy and sexual intimacy in the context of a marriage or a relationship. You can't experience sexual intimacy without there being an emotional connection. If you want to enjoy better sex, you have to work on strengthening the emotional bonds you share, and the more you connect sexually, the stronger your feelings for each other will become. Your bodies and hearts are intricately connected.

Think back to when you and your partner began to realize you were falling for each other. If you consider things carefully, you'll realize the first thing that happened was that you became emotionally vulnerable with each other, having lost your fear of being criticized, mocked, judged, or silenced for being your authentic self. The first time you got naked with each other, you still had your clothes on. How's that possible? You bared your hearts to each other. You said to each other, "Hey, this is all of me, no frills, no masks, and no costumes." From this position, you can create a powerful relationship where you understand and value each other.

Right now, things may not be looking good on the sexual front, but it is possible to sort that out, especially if you've begun working to restore your emotional intimacy by using the exercises from the previous chapter.

Worksheet: Understanding Your Desires and Boundaries

There are a few steps you have to take before you and your partner can be warmed up enough to try sexual intimacy and continue the process of building it. Both of you must do some self-reflection to find out exactly what you need from the other person sexually and what boundaries you have that you'd prefer to be respected. The purpose of this particular worksheet is to encourage self-reflection regarding your sexual desires. Answer the following questions honestly and in as much detail as you can manage in your journal, and discuss your answers with each other when you've finished. This worksheet is a powerful tool to help you and your significant other communicate openly and constructively about these essential matters that hold the key to reigniting the passion between you.

Part 1: Reflecting on Your True Desires

1. When you reflect on your needs and desires in the bedroom, what are the things you love to do that make you feel satisfied?

2. What emotions would you rather feel to help you get in the mood and appreciate the afterglow?

3. Do you have specific preferences, dos and don'ts, and fantasies that you feel would make a sexual connection with your partner more satisfying?

4. Consider every sexual experience you've had in the past, whether with your partner or someone else. Now you have these experiences in mind, what was it about them that you enjoyed, and what do you think you could do to make them happen with your partner?

5. Still recalling your most memorable sexual experiences, what did you hate about them? Is there anything that reminds you of those cringe or uncomfortable moments when you're with your partner sexually? How can you communicate with your partner to stop those things or reach a compromise if your partner gets off on them?

Part 2: Discovering, Clarifying, and Communicating Boundaries

1. What are some of the activities you and your partner have been engaged in sexually in the past that make you feel uncomfortable? List them all, and if you can explain why, do so. If not, that's fine, too.

2. What sort of behavior or sexual activity is an absolute no-no for you?

3. What could your partner do to make you feel like they truly value and respect you before, during, and after your sexual connection?

4. What are some concerning things from your past sexual encounters with your partner (or someone else) that have you worried or afraid, unable to be in the moment and enjoy yourself?

5. What are the things that trigger you badly, whether it's something said or done? List them, and if you'd like to go into detail on each point, do so.

Nurturing a Safe and Intimate Space for Sexual Intimacy

The safer you and your partner feel with each other, the more likely it will be that you'll develop sexual intimacy once more. Remember, you can only be sexually intimate with your partner if both of you are willing to put yourselves in vulnerable positions. However, it is tough to be vulnerable when you feel threatened. So, the point of the following exercises is to help you feel more at ease exploring each other 's bodies and ideas around sexuality. First, here's a look at the many advantages of taking time to create an environment that feels safe for you.

Your willingness to be vulnerable makes it easier to forgive. Your partner will open up as you communicate through words and actions that it is safe to be with you. You, in turn, will be touched by their willingness to be vulnerable. From this space, you can be more honest about your feelings. Even when you assume you've been doing a good job of letting go of the resentment and pain you feel every time you think about your partner and what they did, you may be surprised to find a few sneaky demons are left haunting your thoughts. From this place of safety, you'll be surprised to find the actual insecurities responsible for the few moments when you slip up and say something cutting or feel terrible about this other person. The moments these truths come to light, you can let them go, and you'll be delighted to discover a newer level of closeness with your partner.

Pleasure boosts the speed at which you regain your trust in each other. As you discover the delight of touching each other and feel the warmth that floods your chest as you remember how your partner knows exactly what you like, you'll feel encouraged to trust them more. When you respond to your partner's touch, you make them feel more confident that you love them, and they realize what you share is very precious. Physical and sexual intimacy are about giving and receiving. When it's obvious to each of you that you do want to give the other person pleasure and you would appreciate the pleasure they offer you, you are spurred on to break down any other walls that may still be between you two. Sex is a spiritual act that causes two souls to become one in the moment, and there is no way to let that happen without trust. It is the ultimate act of vulnerability between couples.

You can share the things words can't convey. The truth about emotions, especially in the context of a relationship that is clawing its way back from the abyss it's been plunged into by infidelity, is that they are far too deep and complex to be expressed with words. So, as you work together to create an environment that feels safe and will encourage intimacy, you'll find yourself sharing things that no words could adequately capture. It may sound a little woo-woo, but it is a real thing that you can communicate with each other by simply sitting in silence together. Add in the element of touch and sensuality, and you will increase the volume of the message you're passing along to each other. What's the result? You develop new depths of emotional connection, making it impossible to sever yourselves from each other.

As you communicate with each other in this safe space, your sensuality grows. When your relationship is hit with infidelity, you'll find you no longer feel connected to your partner and are unwilling to explore your sensual side with them, or anyone else for that matter. The way to fix this is to be in a safe space to share your thoughts, feelings, and, eventually, bodies with each other freely. You'll become incredibly sensual once more, and if you make a point of affirming each other by saying things like, "I really like that," or "I love it every time you..." you'll watch your sensuality boom, the walls between you crash, and your hearts blend to become one.

You'll find yourselves desiring each other again. It's one thing to wait for your partner to initiate sexual contact and then respond to it. It's another thing entirely to be unable to wait for them and seek them out yourself. That's what will happen when you both put in the work to create a safe, nurturing space to explore sexual intimacy with each other once more. The more you do it, the more you'll be rewarded with oxytocin, serotonin, and dopamine, and you'll naturally seek out your partner to continue to get a fix. Now, talking about what happens from a chemical perspective is not the most romantic thing on the planet, but if you keep your focus on how that chemical process plays out behaviorally, you'll find that it's worth putting in the time to become hopelessly bound to each other once more, desperate to feel one another every chance you get and, in every way, possible.

You'll develop emotional safety with each other, which is a signal that you're sexually liberated with each other. The problem with the anxiety and insecurity that comes after infidelity is that you and your partner will have a massive problem with spontaneously expressing yourself. If in the past you had no trouble giving one another spontaneous hugs, kisses, and "love taps" on your behinds as you pass by, you now find yourself having to hold back. So, as you develop a safe space where you can communicate honestly and genuinely show each other how hurt you are and how much you want to fix things, you will eventually find yourselves feeling emotionally safe. You'll experience that safety in the bedroom. You'll feel liberated. You'll be willing to do things that, in the past, you probably never thought you could ever do again. So, as you approach the process of rebuilding your sexual intimacy from this state of emotional security, you will find yourselves being willing to explore with no embarrassment. Nothing is more joyful than being spontaneous and free to know that no one will judge you for your choices or what you like. This is why taking the time to set the tone is essential.

Sensory Reconnection Exercise

After you and your partner have chosen a time and space where you know you won't be interrupted (freeing you to let things progress naturally), you must begin by reminding yourself what *feeling each other is like*. That means you have to awaken your senses. The point of this exercise is to help you and your partner find your bond once more through your sensory perception. You can't just rush right into having sex with each other after you've experienced such a rip between you. By slowly exploring each other and titillating your senses, you can gradually reintroduce the idea of safety and security to the bedroom.

Instructions

Gather some materials to help you and your partner explore your senses. Here are a few things you should consider:

1. For **audio,** you'll need to have a speaker and a playlist prepared. It's best to choose a genre of music you both enjoy that will encourage a romantic, soft mood.

2. For **smell,** get perfumes, essential oils, scented candles, and bath bombs. Check to ensure the essential oils are dermatologically tested and skin-friendly.

3. For **sight,** you should both choose to wear something appealing, and you can decorate the space you'll be in with flowers, special lighting, or whatever else can make the place look aesthetically pleasing.

4. Get massage oils, feathers, and soft materials like silk or velvet for **touch.**

5. You'll need some beverages (something you both like), fruit, and snacks for **taste.**

Pick somewhere comfy and safe. If you have kids, it's best to have them be elsewhere for the time being, or you may want to plan a getaway to somewhere special. Set up the room so it's cozy and intimate to focus on each other without distractions. Wherever you are, set everything you need in place so there's no need to keep trooping out of the room to get one thing or another. You want to avoid being unprepared so the mood isn't ruined.

Begin by breathing deeply. You don't have to do fancy meditation if you're unfamiliar with the process. First, sit opposite each other. Then, each of you must pay attention to your breathing for a few minutes. When it's clear you're both settled and in the moment, turn your attention to the other person's breathing. You may find your breathing patterns synchronize with each other's. This is a good thing.

First, explore hearing. You can put your playlist on. As you listen to the music, you should take turns describing what the sounds feel like. Music always evokes emotion, so this shouldn't be a problem. Suppose you struggle to find the right emotions. In that case, it's okay to describe the song as a color, an element of weather like the rain, sun, or a typhoon, an experience like a baby's laugh or a first kiss, etc. Do this for a few songs, then listen to each other's voices. Listen to what you love about each other's voice, and complement each other, keeping eye contact as you do. Then, you may listen to more songs or check in with each other to see if you're ready to move on to the next step.

Move on to smell. You can allow the music to keep playing (hopefully, your playlist is a long one, and if it isn't, you've put it on a loop to start over when it's done) while you bring out each of the things you've chosen for the smell sensory experience. Take turns smelling each scent, and talk about how they make you feel, affect your mood, what or who they remind you of, etc. Sometimes, smells will hit you differently after a second or third check, so be willing to breathe them in again to truly understand what the other person is sharing with you about how the smell affects them. When you've finished experiencing all the smells, move closer to each other and try to pick up on every scent you can, from cologne to aftershave, to perfumes and oils, to natural musk.

Take it all in without saying anything for a while, and then when you're ready, share with the other person what you appreciate about their smell, whether it's the comfort you get from its familiarity or something else. Ensure you hold eye contact as you talk about this.

Move on to the visuals. You can start by taking in the things you've brought to make the room visually pleasing. Talk about how you feel about them, taking turns to share your thoughts and asking questions where you'd like clarification. Become curious about the other person's perspective. Then, when you've finished looking at everything else, it's time to focus on the other person.

Take each other in, noticing everything from how your partner's dressed to how they've styled their hair and accessorized, as well as how the colors they've chosen suit them. Offer each other genuine compliments about what you can visually appreciate about each other, keeping eye contact and smiling softly at each other. If you've been taking your time with the exercise so far, you should feel familiar warmth for the other person in your heart.

Now it's time to play with touch. You can start by picking one of the objects you've brought for exploring touch. Feel that item with your hands or against your face, then describe how it feels to your partner. Have them do the same thing with you. You can use these items to touch the other person, avoiding direct skin contact for now. At this point, ask each other if they notice a difference between when they felt the material alone and when you used it to touch them.

When you finish each item, it's time to touch each other. Reach out and hold hands while keeping your gaze locked on the other person's eyes. Don't move your hands right away. Simply keep their hands in yours. As you hold hands, take turns describing the other person's hands, from texture to temperature, pressure, etc. Then, take turns describing your emotions as you hold each other's hands, focusing on the present. After a while, you can move on to gently rubbing each other's hands, still describing your feelings and any beautiful memories that well up in your mind. Play with the speed and pressure; be playful, be gentle.

Don't thumb your nose at this: Try to emote with your hands. Imagine you're sending your partner a feeling of love and appreciation through your hands to theirs and their heart. Don't think about what that will look like. Instead, allow your hands to do what they will. They know how to pass the message along. You can also smile or gaze lovingly at the other person before you tell them you appreciate them for being so committed to your relationship that they're here, with you, doing this exercise.

If you're both feeling up to it, you can check in with each other to see if you're both open to hugging and holding each other. There's nothing sexual going on here, at least, not yet, and not if you're both not feeling up to it. However, don't be surprised to find that you both have a ravenous desire to be close to each other in every way imaginable at this point in the exercise. If you can turn the lights down lower, that's great. If not, don't sweat it. Just bask in the feeling of being in each other's arms, listening to the music, smelling your combined scents, taking in the moment visually, and being in the here and now with your forever person.

There's no stopping now if you both sense a desire for more intimacy, whether through kisses, caresses, or something more. Surrender to the beauty of being vulnerable with another human, of rediscovering your love and trust for each other once more. It's a rebirth of your love. Nothing from the past exists. This is a new first for you both, one that leads to a glorious life full of love, laughter, light, and joy. If you're not keen on connecting sexually yet, that's fine, too. You could also take turns massaging each other. That's why you have the oil, isn't it? Try to keep it non-sexual unless you both desire more and consent to taking things to the next level. Being consistent with this exercise will eventually lead you both to a place of safety and willingness to try again. The fact that you've both arrived at this point is still causing you to hope for better and, eventually, celebrate your newfound spark.

Now, experiment with taste. Take turns describing the foods, snacks, and whatever else to each other. It's okay not to be fond of how something tastes. Be honest in sharing and describing the food (and please be kind if your significant other took the time to prepare it). This is a chance to have fun, unwind, and enjoy yourselves.

It's time to reflect on how this exercise made you feel. What was it like for you? Take turns sharing, and while you're at it, address the matter of feeling connected and safe with each other, even if it's only been for these few moments. Talk about how to make this a ritual (how often will you do this, during what times, at what location, etc.), and brainstorm ideas to make the next session more interesting.

Finally, thank each other. Let the other person know how much you appreciate their willingness to try to reclaim the relationship. Thank them for choosing to be here rather than anywhere else and fully present with you. They should also tell you how much they appreciate your time and effort. As you wrap up your thanks, verbally commit to making this happen and let the other person know you're looking forward to the next session. Also, plan to bring one "surprise" element to the next one so you both have something to look forward to. It doesn't have to be something elaborate. It only needs to be interesting. This is your chance to break down walls because whatever you choose could have a humorous, revealing, and vulnerable backstory, bringing you closer to each other than ever.

21 Conversational Prompts to Elevate Your Sexual Intimacy

Do you want to be clear about your sexual needs with your partner? Want to know what they'd love from you? How would you like to establish firm, unquestionable boundaries that make you respect each other even more and fall even deeper in love as a result? Use the following prompts. Get ready to be emotionally naked with each other as you answer.

1. "How did infidelity affect the way you feel about the sexual connection we have with each other?"

2. "What can I do to help you feel safer and give you confidence in our love and sexual relationship?"

3. "Is there something I do or say that you'd rather I didn't because they make you remember terrible things from the past or leave you feeling awkward and uncomfortable?"

4. "Do you have any idea how we could have even more trust and vulnerability in the sexual aspect of our relationship with each other?"

5. "Are there better ways we can let each other know what we need and want from each other sexually?"

6. "Can we come up with boundaries for both of us that will always help us feel safe and satisfied with each other in our sexual interactions?"

7. "Are there some things you'd love to try sexually and things you'd rather steer clear of? Please share."

8. "In what ways can we keep our sexual relationship feeling like it's safe for each person and as a couple?"

9. "Do you have any idea how we can encourage a deeper physical and emotional connection between each other? Please share."

10. "Would you be open to working with a professional, like a therapist or a counselor, to help us maneuver our way to deeper levels of sexual intimacy?"

11. "What ideas do you have for staying honest and open with each other about our feelings, thoughts, and experiences of our sexual relationship from now on?"

12. "In what ways is our sexual relationship different from how it used to be before it got hit with infidelity?"

13. "What ideas do you have for how we can keep our sexual relationship fresh, fun, invigorating, and satisfying?"

14. "What do you honestly feel each time we are sexually intimate with each other?"

15. "What things turn you on the most each time we make love, whether it's a specific word or something we do?"

16. "When we're sexually intimate, what makes you feel comforted and loved?"

17. "Do you have any ideas on how we can give our sexual relationship a higher priority than we have in the past? Please share your thoughts."

18. "Could you tell me what I can do to make you feel deeply desired and wanted?"

19. "Outside the context of sex, in what ways can I demonstrate my love and affection for you?"

20. "What are your genuine thoughts about how sexually connected and intimate we are with each other?"

21. "What strategies can we put in place to fan the flames of our sexual connection so it burgeons stronger and better with time?"

Other Activities for Developing Sexual Intimacy

The following are excellent things to incorporate into your love life right away to see the sparks fly and your hunger for each other become powerfully unstoppable.

1. **Read Erotic Literature Together.** Not a fan of reading? No problem. You can both listen to erotic audiobooks. Are you both fancy with words? How about writing some of your own erotica, which you can read to each other? At best, you'll turn each other on. At worst, you'll have a good laugh over any ridiculous bits. If you're laughing, please keep it good-natured. If you're the one being teased, please have a sense of humor and take it in good spirits. Play is a lovely segue to sex, you know.

2. **Groom Each Other** — no, not like cats, unless you're trying to get a laugh or that's your thing. You could share shower time with each other, helping each other clean up. This is a lovely way to be close to each other, and there's no better demonstration of care than literally caring for the other person's body.

3. **Share Your Fantasies.** Then, see how you can make them come true. You have to be tender and respectful of each other here because often, people feel vulnerable about talking about these things. So, you and your partner should declare your space a safe zone where you can talk about these things without fear. Go the extra mile by seeing how you can please each other unless engaging in said fantasy would breach your boundaries. In that case, you can come to a workable agreement with each other.

4. When you're sexually intimate with each other, **Use Your Words and Body Language to Encourage Each Other.** Do this, especially when your partner does something you like. Also, check in with each other the whole time. You're making love, which means it's not about getting yours and getting done. It's about fulfilling the other person's needs, too.

5. **Switch up the Locations** where you both get intimate with each other. Novelty is great for reigniting dying embers every time. Speaking of novelty, what else can you switch up?

6. **Don't Shy Away from Accessories, Props, and Toys** — unless you find them highly uncomfortable or triggering. Don't let your unfamiliarity with these things keep you from trying them out. You may like some things and laugh at others, but either way, they can make things more fun and exciting for you and your lover.

7. **Earn an Oscar — by Role-Playing.** You and your partner can embody other characters to bring back the mystery and excitement between you. Discuss this before you attempt to be someone else for the day or night because your partner may not catch on or be in the mood. It's also good to let them know because you could both develop backstories and scripts for the characters you'll assume. Set a day and a time for this, as well as a signal for when you both know you're done with acting. While it's role-playing, it should be taken seriously. If one of you keeps slipping out of character, it could kill the mood or make things feel too absurd for you to enjoy yourselves. You can have all the laughs you want with each other after the night is over. For fun, you could award each other makeshift Oscars after.

Before moving on from this chapter, please remember you and your partner need to be patient with each other as you work through your sexual intimacy issues. Keep your hearts and minds open. What can you do when you feel a strong push against opening yourself up to your partner? Stay curious. When you think you don't want to engage, pause to ask yourself, "Do I really not want to? Why?" This is how you determine the subconscious blocks to sexual intimacy that stop you from letting that wall crumble. Talk to your partner about it, and see how you can convince yourself to at least be curious about the process (while respecting all boundaries, yours and your partner's). If you approach the process of bringing back the spark with curiosity, your heart and mind will be less defensive.

Chapter 8: Extra Tips for a Positive Outcome

By this point in the book, you should be feeling optimistic about your prospects. You should know that it is possible to revive your relationship and make it even better than it was in the beginning. This chapter aims to give you even more tips that will increase the chances of a positive outcome for your relationship. It is not impossible for you to be in love with this person again and be willing to share your heart, body, and soul with them. All you need is to commit to the process of rescuing your relationship from the jaws of infidelity. You both have to put in effort and support each other because you won't always feel like you can pull it off. During those times, what will help you pull through is a little more patience and understanding. Once you both accept that you can give your relationship a second wind, you are more than halfway through the battle.

The goal is to share your heart, body, and soul with your partner.
https://www.pexels.com/photo/goal-lettering-text-on-black-background-5598296/

Tips for Setting Positive and Realistic Intentions

An excellent way to ensure that you will achieve your goal of recovering your relationship is by keeping your intentions positive and also rooting them in reality. While it is good to hope for the best, you must be realistic about what you can accomplish within any time frame. The human heart is a complicated thing, and so is the mind, so it would be unfair and unrealistic of you to put a time limit on your partner, expecting them to recover within that period. It would also be unfair to yourself. With that out of the way, as long as you both remain committed to the cause, you will achieve progress.

If you want to improve the odds of recovery, you should reframe the process by thinking of it as a never-ending journey of love and dedication to each other. There is no endpoint to this process because there isn't any point at which you love someone "enough" and, therefore, no longer have to show your love. Love, in the context of a relationship, is meant to be a lifelong commitment, so if you are looking at rebuilding after infidelity through this lens, you should have no trouble remaining committed. The correct answer to "How long will this take?" is forever, or at least for as long as you intend to remain together as a couple. So, how can you set the best intentions for your connection, keeping them positive and achievable?

As individuals, find out what your core values are. Core values are everything that you hold in high esteem in life. These are the things that drive you. They inform your boundaries and motivate you to make things happen. These values are non-negotiable. Otherwise, they wouldn't be core values. Take time to reflect on your life and discover the things that you hold dear. When you know what matters to you, you and your partner can get together and see how your values align with each other's. After finding the synergy between both perspectives, you can use your newfound knowledge to drive your intentions and actions toward restoring and growing your relationship. Since you'll both be acting based on your inner values, there is a lower chance of doing anything to jeopardize your union ever again. You'll be proactive about keeping your relationship healthy and happy.

Go beyond simply fixing your connection. Remember, your relationship is meant to last for as long as you're together, which, if you're like normal couples, is for all the time you both have together on earth. In that case, you shouldn't only be looking for how to patch up the holes in your relationship. Your drive should be towards creating a future you can both look forward to enjoying together. If you are only committed to fixing the damage that has been caused by infidelity, you risk stagnating your relationship. Once you attain that goal, there's nothing further to aspire to, and that could be a recipe for disaster. Another reason you should reach for something loftier than mere repair is if you shoot for the moon and miss, you will at least land among the stars. In other words, you will do more than repair your relationship since you'd have to have sorted that out already before you can accomplish the goal of growing as a couple and loving each other more as time passes.

Worksheet: Powerful Intentions for Real Results

Use this worksheet to help you and your partner figure out the things that matter to you the most so you have a better shot at healing your connection after infidelity and doing even more than that.

Part 1: Value and Vision

1. Write down five or ten of your core values in your journal. These values should be centered on your relationships and life in general. For instance, you may value loyalty, openness, honesty, intimacy, communication, etc.

2. Pause for a few minutes to consider the way infidelity affected your perception of your values and how you see yourself. Then, note your observations in your journal.

3. Take some time to think about the future you would love to have regarding your relationship with your partner while working your core values in the mix. Then, as honestly as you can, write about what you desire from your relationship with your partner in the future.

4. From a place of sincerity, fully commit yourself to fixing your relationship and then some. Write about your dedication to the cause. To give your commitment more potency, list at least three things you will do for yourself for the sake of your relationship.

Part 2: The Connecting Thread between Intentions

1. Share your list of core values with each other, and then talk about them. Find the places where you see them connect and where they diverge. Then, talk about how you can compromise with the values that differ (unless these values are clearly on opposite ends of the spectrum, in which case things won't work out), and use your common values to grow your relationship.

2. Now, share the vision that you both have for your future as a couple. The goal of this conversation is to look for the ways in which you see things the same and build on those commonalities.

3. Put your thinking caps on and figure out goals that are attainable and measurable, which will ultimately lead you to the vision that you have for your relationship in the future. Please note that as you make these plans, you must also consider each individual's goals.

4. Discuss your perceptions of what makes communication honest and open. When you have finished, you both have to draw up a plan to encourage this honesty to help your relationship become all it can be.

Worksheet: Finding Gems and Fortifying Your Fortress

Every relationship has its strengths. If you can find yours and build on them, you make it easier to recover your healthy, loving selves once more. Use this worksheet to help you find the good and fortify your love for each other.

Part 1: The Gems You Share

1. Do this step individually. You each have to come up with at least five (at most, ten) experiences you've had with your partner that you cherish the most. You should also write five to ten qualities you think are admirable about your relationship.

2. Swap lists with each other. After going through the other person's lists, take turns talking about each entry. Your goal is to discuss this in a celebratory way so you can both appreciate that you have something beautiful going on here.

3. Then, take turns talking about unique obstacles and challenges you've experienced and have triumphed over as a couple. A

good talking point would be how these obstacles somehow revealed the strengths and positives you carried within you as individuals and couples.

Part 2: Fortifying Your Love

1. As a team, revisit your list of strengths and positives, and choose three to five of the ones you deem most important to developing a healthy relationship that stands the test of time.

2. Next, you both have to brainstorm. What new habits can you start to help these strengths become even stronger? Are there certain things you can do right away and consistently to make these positive pillars of your relationship even more prominent and secure?

3. Discuss the issues you think could stand in the way of your love becoming stronger – honestly and openly. Get it all on paper. When you've done that, you have to come together and strategize ways to keep these weak links in your relationship from breaking on you and ruining what you've built so far.

4. Now it's time to consider how you will both be supportive of each other when the storms of life hit your relationship. Talk about how you handle everything from disagreements to pressure from the outside, from health issues to financial ones, etc.

5. The next step is to schedule time every week or month when you check in with each other to see how you're progressing on the journey of developing a stormproof relationship. Commit to showing up for each other during these check-ins and implementing the action plans you come up with each time.

6. Thank each other for participating in this exercise as a team and following through with the homework you've received.

Why You Need Constant Self-Reflection and Personal Growth

In any relationship, if one or both parties don't bother with self-reflection and do anything to achieve personal growth, that relationship is doomed to fail. Two people make up this union, and to achieve the heights it can, both must be proactive about becoming better versions of themselves. How can you become a better version of yourself if you don't take the time to reflect on your choices and your current position in life so far?

Self-reflection is also essential because you will continue to evolve as you mature. There is no way around this process. It never ends. Your passions will change, and so will your values. Once upon a time, you may have dreamed of this, and now you dream of that because, over time, your desires have subtly shifted. If you aren't consciously tracking these changes within yourself, you'll wake up one day and feel utterly lost and confused about how you got where you are. "Lost and confused" is not a good state to be in for your relationship. So, as you practice constant self-reflection through journaling and contemplation, you'll discover your new needs and if these are being met. If they aren't, you can share what you've learned with your partner, and both of you can sort that out. The same applies to the other person in the relationship, of course.

Letting Helping Hands Help

While the relationship is between you and one other person, the fact remains that there will be times when you will need support. You may feel confused about some issues, and it helps to have an outside perspective to help you gain clarity. For instance, if you ever find yourself in a position where you're not feeling appreciative of your partner or your connection with them, someone on the outside could help you look at things differently and help you find the love in your heart for your significant other once more. They do this while validating your feelings, of course, but in the same breath, they will gently nudge you to see the good that you have. Friends and family can remind you that there is no such thing as a perfect relationship, and the grass will always be greener where you water it. They also have their experiences to draw on to offer you helpful insights on how to handle obstacles or challenges.

Your friends and family should always be involved in your relationship to an appropriate extent because they are people who typically share the same values as you do. You wouldn't be connected to them if you didn't have the same set of morals. So, you can think of these people as enforcers and reinforcers who ensure that your relationship continues to toe the line of those values and morals that you hold dear. It's also nice to know that in times of trouble, you can draw security and strength from the people who have known and loved you most of your life. They'll be there to cheer you on through the worst of times until you and your partner can make it out into the sunlight again. Also, if there's ever a curveball thrown at you, one that is too tough and heavy to bear on your own, these people, your friends and family will become your sanctuary. They will give you unwavering support and console you without judgment.

Conclusion

This book may have concluded, but a new chapter of your relationship has just begun. How the story ends is entirely up to you and your partner. The fact that you've read to this point is a clear indicator that you are not willing to give up on your relationship despite infidelity and its horrible effects. This is a good sign you'll pull it off in due time. You don't have to wait for the worst of times to hit before you do all you can to reinforce the positive in your relationship. With that said, it's helpful to reflect regularly on all the beautiful moments you and your partner have shared. In fact, you should go so far as to create a schedule for this sort of positive reflection. Why is this essential? Because as you constantly recall all the good things about being together, you're depositing good vibes into an emotional bank account of sorts that you can draw from when things get challenging.

The last thing you need is to struggle with a particularly bad day (or a fresh challenge) just to find your emotional bank account in the red. There is no such thing as "doing too much" when you're rescuing your relationship from doom. Refusing to put in the effort will only leave you wondering in the future if you could have done more. It is much better to know that you did all you could to keep love's flame ablaze in both your hearts.

While the tips and strategies offered in this book are created in a linear fashion, you have to recognize that healing a relationship is not a linear process. There will be ups, and there will be downs. That's the way it goes, like it or not. So rather than allow yourself to live a Pollyanna life or buy into the Disney fantasy where everything works out happily ever after with no effort on either person's part, it is much better to be prepared and brace up for the hard times to come. There's no escaping the difficult times. However, as long as you both are committed to seeing things through, it's only a matter of time before the rain stops falling and the sunshine bursts through the clouds of your relationship.

Don't spend every waking moment worrying about the tough times. Instead, be on the lookout for every little sign of progress you can detect. When you see that you and your partner are making headway with specific challenges, you owe it to each other and your relationship to pause and celebrate that with all your heart. Make a big deal out of it. Why? Because it is a big deal. Each and every sign of improvement is a cheerleader yelling at you to keep going, telling you that the light of true love, openness, honesty, vulnerability, and all the other beautiful values of a healthy relationship is ready to shine on you both. Your mutual celebration will remind you during challenges that you can't quit now because you've come so far! You deserve love in its truest form — and with time, patience, commitment, and understanding, you'll look back on this dark time one day, and it will feel like such a distant memory it could very well be someone else's life.

References

Afifi, W.A., Falato, W.L., & Weiner, J.L. (2001). Identity Concerns Following a Severe Relational Transgression: The Role of Discovery Method for the Relational Outcomes of Infidelity. Journal of Social and Personal Relationships

Apostolou, M., & Panayiotou, R. (2019). The Reasons That Prevent People from Cheating on Their Partners: An Evolutionary Account of the Propensity Not to Cheat. Personality and Individual Differences

Baskin, T.W., & Enright, R.D. (2004). Intervention Studies on Forgiveness: A Meta-Analysis. Journal of Counseling & Development

Beltrán-Morillas, A.M., Valor-Segura, I., & Expósito, F. (2019). Unforgiveness Motivations in Romantic Relationships Experiencing Infidelity: Negative Affect and Anxious Attachment to the Partner as Predictors. Frontiers in Psychology

Burnette, J.L., & Franiuk, R. (2010). Individual Differences in Implicit Theories of Relationships and Partner Fit: Predicting Forgiveness in Developing Relationships. Personality and Individual Differences

Edwards, T., Pask, E.B., Whitbred, R., & Neuendorf, K.A. (2018). The Influence of Personal, Relational, and Contextual Factors on Forgiveness Communication Following Transgressions. Personal Relationships

Finkel, E.J., Burnette, J.L., & Scissors, L.E. (2007). Vengefully Ever After: Destiny Beliefs, State Attachment Anxiety, and Forgiveness. Journal of Personality and Social Psychology

Glass, S., & Staeheli, J. C. (2007). NOT "Just Friends": Rebuilding Trust and Recovering Your Sanity After Infidelity. Free Press.

Harley, W. F., & Jennifer Harley Chalmers. (1998). Surviving an Affair. Fleming H. Revell.

John Mordechai Gottman, & Silver, N. (2013). What Makes Love Last? : How to Build Trust and Avoid Betrayal. Simon & Schuster Paperbacks.

Kirshenbaum, M. (2008). When Good People Have Affairs. Macmillan.

Snyder, D. K., Baucom, D. H., & Kristina Coop Gordon. (2007). Getting Past the Affair: A Program to Help You Cope, Heal, and Move On -- Together or Apart. Guilford Press.

Solomon, S. D., & Teagno, L. J. (2006). Intimacy after Infidelity: How to Rebuild and Affair-Proof Your Marriage. New Harbinger Publications.

Thompson, A. E., Capesius, D., Kulibert, D., & Doyle, R. A. (2020). Understanding Infidelity Forgiveness: An Application of Implicit Theories of Relationships. Journal of Relationships Research, 11, Article e2

Weiner-Davis, M. (2017). Healing from infidelity: the Divorce Busting Guide to Rebuilding Your Marriage After an Affair. Michele Weiner-Davis Training Corporation.